DREAMS OF

BEING EATEN ALIVE

DREAMS OF BEING EATEN ALIVE

The Literary Core of the Kabbalah

DAVID ROSENBERG

Harmony Books
New York

Published by Harmony Books, 201 East 50th Street, New York,
New York 10022. Member of the Crown Publishing Group.

Random House, Inc. New York, Toronto, London, Sydney, Auckland
www.randomhouse.com

HARMONY BOOKS is a registered trademark and Harmony Books
Colophon is a trademark of Random House, Inc.

Printed in the United States of America

Design by Sue Maksuta

Library of Congress Cataloging-in-Publication Data
Rosenberg, David, 1943–
Dreams of being eaten alive : the literary core of the kabbalah /
David Rosenberg — 1st ed.
p.   cm.
Includes bibliographical references.
I. Cabala—History and criticism.   I. Title.
BM526.R67   2000
296.I'6—dc2I   99-41901
                                                    CIP

ISBN 0-609-60306-X
10   9   8   7   6   5   4   3   2   I
First Edition

to Rhonda

"The sorrow of interrupted life is nothing compared to the sorrow of interrupted study. The probability that the former may continue beyond the grave seems infinite when compared to the inexorable incompletion of the latter."

V. Nabokov

C O N T E N T S

9

ACKNOWLEDGMENTS

Fifteen years ago, in the Jerusalem home of Gershom Scholem, I was invited by Fanya, his widow, to study his unpublished notebooks as well as marginalia on texts of the Kabbalah, in my capacity as editor of the Jewish Publication Society. At the dining room table, in the presence on all sides of the shelved volumes of personal notations, I gained entry to a conversation still in progress with the Kabbalah. I'm thankful as well for particularly moving chats with Harold Schimmel, Ronit Meroz, Rabbis Adin Steinsaltz and Gedaliah Fleer, Shalva Segal, Susan Afterman, and the late poets Allen Afterman and Dennis Silk in Jerusalem; Michal Govrin in Jerusalem and New York; Moshe Idel in Jerusalem, New York, and New Haven; Harold Bloom in New York and New Haven; David Shapiro and Rabbi Moshe Shur in New York; and the late Isaac Bashevis Singer in New York and Miami. I'm also grateful for the privileges granted me in the Jewish Collections of the libraries at Oxford University, Jewish Theological Seminary, New York University, Hebrew Union College in Jerusalem, the Hebrew University of Jerusalem, and the University of Miami. My radiant editor Shaye Areheart, Dina Siciliano, Nina Rothberg, and Laura Wood contributed mightily, as did Lew Grimes and

Walter Brown, friends and agents of many realms. Most significantly, the chapter "Receiving the Kabbalah" was coauthored with Rhonda Rosenberg. Beyond that, it's safe to say that this book would not have seen the light of day but for the unique interpretive voice she lent to it.

Part I

HOW TO READ THE KABBALAH

I

A question I carried around but never quite asked as an adult: If the Kabbalah is so great, why does it sound so dull when explained or in translation?

A question I carried around but didn't know how to ask in childhood: If sex is so great, why do my parents and most of the adults I know keep it secret? (This might not apply as aptly to children today, who find easy access in the popular culture. Still, the lack of meaningful interpretation continues to beg the question: Why is it so great?)

In my adolescence I became infatuated with poetry, which I hoped would help me win the love of the most intellectual as well as sexy young woman I had ever encountered (we'll leave my mother out of this). She was so much better read than I was that I intended to forestall the revelation of my inferiority by forcing her to read my own cryptic sonnets in place of discussing Shakespeare's. I had at least understood that a paradoxical text would invite more interest or discussion than a clumsy imitation.

So I became a sonneteer of the obscure. I also became a grand failure, which probably ensured that I would continue on the poet's path until I could properly respect my own intelligence. I could not get the girl to speak of my poems at all, and when I finally cornered her, she explained that she would have told me this sooner except she had worried that it would discourage me from writing: she had begun dating the high school's star fullback and beefcake. Once again, lack of a proper understanding of sex had stymied me.

But I was determined to learn it from the primary source available to me in the tenth grade of that puritanical day, namely, my own sexual dreams. My method was to wake up secretly after midnight and attempt to capture those dreams on paper. I found that the dreams were scarier than I thought they would be, and although there was plenty of sex, I could not tell what was happening, as in my sonnets. At this point, I began to read *Portrait of the Artist as a Young Man*, the novel by James Joyce, in my tenth-grade English class, and the revelations began. First, Joyce made all of reality sound like a dream, too. Second, the vision of hell that young Stephen Daedalus encountered sounded similar to my own dream writings.

I began to try to verify my intuition that all of great literature was written as if a dream. I read Artur Rimbaud's *A Season in Hell*, and then the newest books of poetry—Allen Ginsberg's *Howl* and Robert Lowell's *Life Studies*—all of them sounding like fever dreams in which the soul crossed over from the real world into a mirroring world of hell. The same seemed true of the great painter of the day, Jackson Pollock, whose feverish trails of dripping paint seemed to testify to the soul's precarious separation from the body. By this time I was aware of a danger in dreaming—and I was able to connect it to a childhood sense of the danger in words themselves. The word *camp*, for instance.

As a child, I learned that my aunts, uncles, and cousins smiling in the family photo album had "died in the camps," and worse: they were made into soap. Yet I was sent to a camp every summer. My body went to Camp Fresh Air, but my soul could be in danger of going to another camp. My guide through this time proved to be useful again as an adult: the famous Psalm 23, recited at camp and in countless graveside scenes in westerns and war movies. The Lord is my shepherd and I am a sheep. I can follow him anywhere and fear no evil, because my soul will keep walking after death. As if in a dream, my soul will find a table waiting with a full cup, a table set for a person instead of a sheep. Even though this seemed to be a bright ending, the key to the poem for me was that it set the model that dreams were about dying and the fear of being lost or eaten (either fate associated with sheep). But where was the sex? "He maketh me to lie down in green pastures...thy rod and thy staff they comfort me...thou anointest my head with oil; my cup runneth over." Sex was in the body, male or female, which fears and is released from fear by ejaculation.

Does that sound wild, or even blasphemous? We are approaching the method of the Kabbalah. It can only be done if we own up to our dreams, because that is where we learn that the soul has a life of its own, but that it cannot be separated from sex. Nothing less than a major intellectual (and literary) landmark of this century,

Freud's *The Interpretation of Dreams*, bears this out. In place of the soul, Freud posits our interior life or "unconscious," and, like the soul itself, the unconscious is prey to fears of dying and of unconsummated sex. Why should the soul fear death? *Separation anxiety* is the scientific term, but in the Kabbalah it is represented as an uncertain journey, out of the body, that the soul takes every night while we dream. On its ascent, our soul is in danger of being distracted by the "other side," a world of evil that reproduces itself by devouring the human semen that is spilled in the wrong frame of mind (and impregnating the female with this "other" seed, if she is desirous in the wrong frame of mind as well). For both sex and dying, the soul must depend on our having achieved the right frame of mind—and that is what the great intellectual work and literary art of the Kabbalah depends on. Is that not what all great literature is built upon—expressing a satisfying attitude toward those forces beyond our control, namely death and desire? And a fascination with our failure to reach such satisfaction—in other words, a description of hell.

The Kabbalah is obsessed with failed sex, especially the spilling of semen in sleep or masturbation, which is attributed to our unconscious intercourse with Lilith—the female consort of the "other side"—or with Samael, the male aspect of the evil tempter. Again, this imagery proves psychologically valid today in terms of the mind's daily struggle between unsuppressed desires and thoughts. The Kabbalah describes itself as a science of this knowledge, but its literary veracity is what finally made me aware of greatness in the Kabbalah, the great art of its literary core. Yes, it offers meanings, but, of even more relevance today, it presents a way of searching for meaning. It ranges from dreams to fear and desire, putting aside all boundaries and taboos in the search for what is truly alive. Just as it discriminates between thought and desire in the crucible of the sexual act, it is passionate about its enemy: the staving off of deadness, of hatred, and misunderstanding. After all, the Kabbalah was the most vital aspect of Judaism during a time in medieval and Renaissance Europe when the dominant belief was that Judaism had been superseded by Christianity and would die out. Most people, even the most cultured, would have been shocked to realize how hard Judaism was fighting to remain alive and growing, both intellectually and spiritually.

The mystery of the Kabbalah, in terms of its largely unknown literary greatness, lies in its answers to the hard questions I first asked above. If sex or love—that is, desire—is so great, why is it not the object of the greatest intellectual excitement? And if sex or love—or hate—can be so wounding, why must its most hidden knowledge remain secret?

❦

Further questions lead to the dreams at the core of the Kabbalah. They reveal how modern and, more accurately, how postmodern is the central work of kabbalistic art, the *Zohar* (Radiance). How far have we come from the subconscious logic (or dream logic) that if our parents can produce us, they can eat us—a logic represented in the Greek pantheon of gods? Is there an element of fear inspired by a monotheistic creator who, because he made us, can also unmake us? The *Zohar* is unafraid to work through these questions and others, including cannibalism and dismemberment, but the reason we have not heard about these questions before is that they do not offer easy explanations about the central mythology of the Kabbalah.

Most books and articles on the Kabbalah are about explaining and simplifying, which is all well and good. But there has to be a time when the explaining stops and the dreaming begins, when our desire can be free enough to experience its influence on waking thought. This experience has been reported by the Kabbalists, and although they wrote as many as seven centuries ago, they are our first postmodern writers: they frame their explorations of desire in the form of lost books and dramatic accounts from the past.

2

When I think of a reader of the Kabbalah, it is not someone who wants a definition that an encyclopedia can provide. That kind of person (whom most books about the Kabbalah attempt to appease) wants to add the Kabbalah to their accumulation of knowledge. They want to distinguish it from Gnosticism or the Talmud. Perhaps they believe knowledge is power—but the Kabbalah itself would more likely ask, "Power for what?" In doing so, it may seem to have an answer for why most people are drawn to it. They are searching for something still unknown to themselves. Possibly the Kabbalah is it, or it can help. I imagine that what they want the Kabbalah to be is a mystery that rivals those at the bottom of our awareness: the mystery of sex, of death, and of happiness.

How do I tell them what the Kabbalah is if I don't reveal a secret myself? For I brought my own secret to it, and most readers have brought theirs—though unaware of it. It has less to do with finding something and more with losing oneself. Those who don't want the heartbreak of opening this secret proceed to dance around it—and that is how the Kabbalah often appears, as a dance of mystical steps: meditation, trance, numerology, astrology, prayer. But it would be wrong to see the Kabbalah in the dance;

instead, the various dance steps all have a common purpose: to focus the mind in preparation for what comes next. And that is the risking of our mortal soul as it leaves the body temporarily in dreams—or in reading the dreamlike core of the *Zohar*. This concept of risking the soul continues to exist in each of us today, no matter how modern we are, because it is a representation of our interior life.

Why the risk? I thought I knew the answer when I became a published poet. I thought I was one of the elect, the privileged few who lived for the art of this risk. My college writing teachers were Robert Lowell and Delmore Schwartz, both of whom suffered on the edge of madness. The danger came from mirroring the world of our contemporaries, of slipping inside the pulse of the times—and losing yourself. Although it is a commonplace that writers show us who we really are, the poetry to which I aspired went further to critique the cultural platitudes about art itself and throw them in doubt. Yet this was still to be part of a long tradition, dubbed the avant-garde in one era, the underground in another, and in our time termed "outside."

In other words, I wanted to be among those who were still in the forest, scouting the future. I will explain further how this career developed, but my purpose now is to find expression for the Kabbalah. The Hebrew word *kabbalah* suggests tradition, one often described as secret or mystical, a tradition that may be older than the Bible. Both before and during the centuries of the European Renaissance, the Kabbalah flourished in an underground Jewish renaissance of its own, in southern Europe and in the land of Israel. Yet it was primarily underground, in the sense that Jews and the Hebraic-Aramaic language of much of the Kabbalah constituted a marginalized culture; it was only secret to those without the immense learning it required; and it was only mystical to those who read or practiced it literally. The principal text of the Kabbalah was in fact profoundly nonliteral and highly imaginative. The *Zohar* (1281–1290) took the interpretive powers of the earlier Talmud and Midrash (venerable traditions of Jewish biblical interpretation) to new imaginative heights, rivaling any humanistic work of Christian Europe in its own Renaissance a bit later.

The Kabbalah has remained a tradition of great interest to Western culture not because its texts were known, however, but due to rituals and practices (including ways of reading) that were derived from them—and then written about in later books. These practices were described as mystical to suggest their spiritual intuition about our cosmic origins and destination, but in fact their derivation from the *Zohar*—the central text of the Kabbalah—is literal-minded. In other words, the practices do not really face the future but rather dwell on *preparing* to do so. The *Zohar*, on the other hand, is a layered work, written in many genres (including invented conversations among invented scholars) around a literary core; and it asks of its reader a more complicated attention than mysticism alone—not unlike the Bible itself.

The *Zohar* might also be contrasted with *The Divine Comedy* of Dante, written in approximately the same period. Imagine that

23

Dante's great work was known primarily for its medieval theology while the power of its poetry was ignored. A silence about the lavish beauty and art of the *Zohar* reflects this fate, partly imposed by its literal-minded users, but there is also the matter of its unusual language. It appears difficult because its literary core is submerged.

The *Zohar* is purposefully in disguise, and the prime agent of this sublime disguise is an invented language, a hybrid of Aramaic and Hebrew that supports the literary artifice of the text's professed ancient composition. Its primary author, Moses de Leon, in keeping with prophetic tradition, presents the book as a lost and rediscovered text, composed a millennium earlier by a legendary prophet, Rav (Rabbi) Shimon bar Yohai, while he was hiding from the Romans in a cave for thirteen years.

Resembling the composition of the Bible, the *Zohar* and its authors (besides de Leon, other Kabbalists in his circle may have written portions) assimilate many strands of earlier writing and oral tradition—retranslating them, as it were. In the manner that it suggests a prophetic commentary on the Hebrew Bible, the *Zohar* resembles a book of the Midrash (like the Kabbalah, also a library of many books of commentary). The *Zohar*, however, develops an additional layer of myth and cosmology, which allows wider scope for imaginative flight and a return to the creative type of composition that writers of the Bible derived from the mythic life of their time.

It is the layer of kabbalistic myth that is the sole subject of most books about the Kabbalah, and for that reason these books can be misleading. They do not answer or even ask the question of how a great kabbalistic book like the *Zohar* could be written—of how the artistic genius of its authors worked. Though the myth may be in some sense expanded by mystical inspiration, great books require a writer's inspiration. Even when the *Zohar* can be viewed in terms of a kabbalistic *process* of composition, assimilating many layers, it is the author's literary vision that holds it together.

The *Zohar* transforms the superstitions and legends it absorbs into a higher art. Yet many of these superstitions remain alive apart from the Kabbalah itself and are often confused with it. The heavenly world of angels and its dark side of demons are especially prone to literal interpretation, instead of the *Zohar's* more complicated projection of our interior life—in the form of the soul—and its struggle for balance.

The *Zohar's* concern with the soul, with unconscious and preconscious life, pits it against the preoccupation with society and personality that literature usually addresses. So the *Zohar* becomes a critique of the status quo and of conventional society. Ahead of the European Renaissance, the *Zohar* tips the balance in favor of a new kind of individuality. Each Kabbalist can himself become a tremendously unique individual in his own writings, as he projects his struggle to balance inner and outer worlds. Were intellectual women to have found a place in this exclusive world of men, its creativity might have ranged even further.

3

But what is a Kabbalist today? He or she is unlikely to be found in a university or a normative religious school. Why not? A Kabbalist does not teach *about* Kabbalah; instead, he or she expresses it. Would he be an artist, then? That would be partly true: a Kabbalist would be part artist and part scientist, just as the Renaissance Kabbalist was often part visionary and part philosopher. Which science? The frontier sciences, those that are pushing forward toward understanding greater complexity. In the early part of this century, the frontier might have been a hybrid of physics and psychology, both of them delving deeper into the hidden complexity of matter and mind. But today, at the end of the century, the forward-most science, as declared by writers and scientists as dissimilar as Edward O. Wilson and Stephen Jay Gould, is evolutionary ecology. Gould describes ecosystem science by quoting D'Arcy Thompson on microbiology half a century ago: "We have come to the edge of a world of which we have no experience, and where all our preconceptions must be recast." (Stephen Jay Gould, *Leonardo's Mountain of Clams and the Diet of Worms: Essays on Natural History*, New York: Harmony Books, 1998, p. 404.)

As ecology is entangled with the complexity of the body, so is the Kabbalah. The *Zohar* seeks to recast our origins by returning to the Garden of Eden, rediscovering it as a place from which not only our body but our soul emanates. Just as the microscope reveals the world of microbes, the invisible soul is unveiled under the lens of a kabbalistic metaphysics—or "system of knowledge"—of our interior life.

But what about the Kabbalah's preoccupation with words? It is not the words themselves, for the text is but a garment, says the *Zohar.* "The core of the garment is the body" and "as the body is clothed in garments, so the stories of the world clothe the Torah." (Zohar 3:152a)

To the Kabbalist, the body is the most complex of entities, mirrored in the Garden of Eden by "the primordial Adam," the original body of Adam before he fell. The entire "body" of kabbalistic myth and cosmology is envisoned as a human body in the image of the Creator and called a Tree of Life. The center of this "tree" of ten *sefirot* (regions of the upper world that reach from man to Creator) is Yesod, the phallus. It was quite evident to a Kabbalist that the body was the most complex of connections to this world, while its interior life (or soul) was connected to the cosmos, the upper world. "All is connected," says the *Zohar.* Concerning the male body, its most complex connection to the natural world is represented by the organ with which it reproduces sexually—and through which it creates the unfolding of human history.

The Kabbalist knew nothing of evolutionary theory, yet his focus on natural and sexual complexity resembles frontier ecology today (as well as the new paradigm that oversimplifies it, known as "deep time"). A reader may wonder how ecology is concerned with myth and cosmology, since it appears to have no interest in the soul and in the upper world. Remember, however, that we are only at the infancy of this new science, and that a correspondence to the soul is already suggested by the science of ecosystems. How? All species, including the human body, evolved in an association with others in its ecosystem so complex—across time and space—that we do not even know how to begin to look at it, let alone accurately describe or measure it. Far more complex than the body itself—and invisible as a complete entity, since it includes microorganisms and regions underground and in the atmosphere—the ecosystem in which humans evolved resembles the soul in relation to the body. Like the soul when it leaves the body, the ecosystem goes through many changes over time but is itself relatively undying.

The Kabbalists grounded their myth in the Garden of Eden. This is an imaginative device posited as true—similar to suggesting that a text the Kabbalist is writing in the present is actually a thousand years old. This is what the central author of the *Zohar* did, making his main character also its "real" author (the messianic figure of Rav Shimon bar Yohai) in the manner that Moses was imagined to have written his own story in the Torah (the Bible's first five books). According to the Kabbalists, the Garden of

Eden and the nature of life in it, including Adam and Eve, is lost to us for now (obscured by our inheritance, the Tree of Knowledge), yet the kabbalistic myth finds ways to recover this lost past—utilizing that other tree in the Garden, the Tree of Life.

How were we different in the Garden of Eden? The *Zohar* assumes our consciousness was cosmic then, stretching from earth to heaven. In today's terms, I would call this cosmic sense of the world "ecological mind," since the word that best suggests cosmic today is *evolutionary*: it includes the prehistory of all life before us as well as all life that will continue to evolve in the future, even after the extinction of our own species, *Homo sapiens*.

At a certain point in my career as a poet and scholar, at the age of thirty, I came to believe that there was no vision of a sustainable future that was worth "clearing the land." For most people today, the future is a grandiose projection of the present, and hopefully free of ideology. But people are also not too curious about much else beyond human culture—as it exists and as it is expected to continue. Space may be interesting, but it will not change us much, as is reflected in the popular mythology of *Star Wars* and *Star Trek*. A better world is generally understood as a healthier, more comfortable life for humans.

This was not a vision that satisfied my soul. Nor is it congenial to most poets, but they have largely turned to examining rather than reimagining the world. Instead, I turned back to a deeper past, to a strange time in which there is much historical and spiritual interest in the vision that was produced—but almost no interest in the writers who produced it. I began to re-study the biblical Hebrew I learned in youth and to retranslate the Hebrew Bible by imagining its human authors. I conceived of it as a type of restoration: instead of clearing the forest for more human culture, I was restoring the wiped-out memory of generations of ancient poets who gave us the early Bible. And since the curious thing about these Hebraic poets is that their vision of the future was more complex than ours today, the question I began to ask myself was: What might such an author write today?

The answer did not become apparent until I encountered the more recent post-biblical writers who were completely turned toward the future while reimagining the past: the Kabbalists, for whom the biblical writers were ancestral. Like other Kabbalists, Moses de Leon was also a "translator," but what were his texts? Since they were largely invented or reimagined, de Leon was a poet of the future, for his character of Shimon bar Yohai predicts not only de Leon's own life to come a millennium after his but the fate of future millenniums. Bar Yohai imagines a future for both the planet and the universe that is remarkably similar to what frontier ecology posits—a future based on a complex series of concepts about balance.

4

In our conventional usage, the terms *soul, world, heaven,* and *hell* depend on a human-centered universe. These terms are already satirized for their self-centeredness in Dante's *The Divine Comedy.* In the *Zohar,* these terms are reinvented to fit a nonhuman universe. The central myth of the Kabbalah turns the entire cosmos into a system—a Tree of Life—in which human life is connected to everything else, including the Creator, in a symbiotic relationship. The soul no longer belongs to a specific person but is suspended between worlds. A mirror universe of the "other side" (or hell) acknowledges the power of disunity (or evil) to be anywhere in the system. But *system* is another term that is oversimplified in common usage.

Similar scientific terms today—for example, *environment, evolution,* or *ecosystem*—have been reduced in popular language to human-centered concepts, even though they were coined to refer to specifically nonhuman realms. As well, the word *Kabbalah* has been diminished by its popular meaning of "secret," or even "mystical."

Most mystical systems follow the old biological model: a "mascot" organism (such as a lion or panda) is surrounded by its habitat. In the same way, the invisible world surrounds the mystic and becomes the habitat for his or her soul.

In recent years, however, evolutionary biology has overturned this model, in an uncanny resemblance to some new trends in mystical and critical thinking. Instead of habitat, we now find ourselves in the more complex model of an ecosystem, in which no single organism is central. How does this new paradigm resemble the Kabbalah, as I've suggested? Instead of the division between finite body and immortal soul, with the latter ascending to its heavenly habitat, the body in Kabbalah remains forever in tension with the upper world, which is interdependent with the lower world in a symbiosis: the soul travels up and down in cycles of regeneration and in new bodies. This stark dependency on balance between body and soul, world and cosmos, resembles an ecosystem in which all species are interrelated.

It is dreams that cross the borders of these worlds, which is why they remain a key to the scientific study of consciousness today. Ecosystems also resemble dreams, in that they encompass many worlds. Foremost in their relation to kabbalistic myth, ecosystems put our bodies into proper perspective.

In ecosystems, everything is food, *including* our bodies. Once, the human line was food for leopards and lions; even today we remain the prey of organisms inside and outside our bodies that invade us and bring us down. Just as a world is hidden within our bodies, there are hidden worlds in a tree, such as the invisible world of microbes. Both our bodies and the trees can be seen now as systems in themselves, interdependent with vast numbers of other species. In the same way, our interior lives (our souls, to the Kabbalist) can be vulnerable to being eaten from within by the social pressures of repression. From repression come contemporary dreams of being eaten alive that parallel the invasion of our dream lives by Lilith and Samael. Also embodied as the snake(s) from Eden (again, with both sexes represented), Lilith and Samael may eat away at our desires as well as devour our semen and babies.

The world of the "other side," which includes Lilith and Samael, is constantly striving to throw the system of our inner and outer worlds out of balance. That is why the Kabbalah is focused upon the intention to unite outer and inner worlds as completely as male and female are in intercourse. This intention is called *yihud*, a drive for union, and is an archetypal picture of sexual reproduction that is projected into the cosmic world until the creation of souls is seen as the offspring of a divine intercourse. The representation of this divine drive for union is surely as old as the monotheistic desire and its exclamation of unity: "God is One."

Now consider the convergence of the Kabbalah with contemporary discoveries. We used to think of our cultures as human habitats, centered upon the human imagination. If the imagination is the capacity of the mind to encompass other forms of life, then, as the modern American poet Wallace Stevens stated ironically, "The world imagined is the ultimate good." Soon this concept of culture will expand further, resembling the intuition of the Kabbalah that all beings and worlds are interconnected beyond imagination. As we begin to understand the details of how each species evolved, it is no longer as easy as it was just a century ago to believe in the individual creation of species. Now the interdependence is becoming clear as we read the history of genes and DNA, with their narratives of ancient relationships and their suggestive poetry about the future.

So it is in the *Zohar:* boundaries of fiction and nonfiction disappear, genres intermarry. Our prehistory in the Garden of Eden is just as vital as our cultural history, if not more so. For the Garden of Eden still exists; it is in our future, depicted in the *Zohar.* It is also a vision of a planet restored to a balance not yet fathomable.

The Kabbalah's Garden of Eden was once a scene of sexual dysfunction that reverberated in the upper world. It was followed by loss of home, an exile. The embedded goal of Kabbalah is to create a new space in which to dwell—not a new house or even land, but an imaginary space in which the latter are viable. How to create new space—that is the question, and it leads to a new text as well, one in which poetry and narrative can become free again, as they were in the early Bible. The *Zohar* is the result. It establishes a new balance between the inner world of soul (and its eventual place in the upper world) and the outer world of body, whose place is in the lower world. Yet the emphasis is not on *place* but on the *balance.*

Everyone faces a personal crisis at some point. Our lives feel too constricted in some way, and for a moment we become sensitized to ways out of time. Art and prayer are two of those ways to get outside of ourselves, although both are products of human culture. How do we find a way out of our *Homo sapiens* limitations for even a moment, in order to see ourselves as temporal creatures from a vantage point beyond time?

The Kabbalah yearns for such a way, and in the past decade so, too, has evolutionary ecology. Both are ways of seeing toward what messianic religion calls "the end of time." In that way, they are also an end to exile. Both the soul's exile in the body—that is, the inner feelings of misunderstood sexual desire—and the human cultural exile from the natural world.

5

After morning coffee in the café at Parrot Jungle next to my home, near the Florida Everglades, the daily heartbreak comes while viewing the many species of tropical plants, birds, primates, and reptiles—in their cages. If the birds and the song of their colors and mouths are morning prayers, then the cages are our hearts. It is not about human cruelty, not just that we imprison them. Rather, it is about the impoverishment of our seeing.

When we see animals in cages or plants in gardens we see aspects of ourselves—aspects that reinforce our superiority as a species. Yes, the articulate hands and feet of lemurs are shocking, more adroit than our own. Yes, the sex organs of mated Ethiopian Borassus palm trees appear more erotically phallic and ovarian than our own. But the nervous stares of birds in their cages remind us of our intelligence—and especially of our inner lives, of which the plants and animals seem dispossessed.

It is no different through the eye of a camera. What we relate to, as in zoos, are the individual or the family group, and this is a hugely distorted picture of the animals in their home ecosystems. Even the plants are different there (as opposed to what we think of as "the wild," which too often means degraded ecosystems). In their ecosystem, each species exists in relation to myriad others, and those others act as an expansion of their intelligence—as antennae, if you will, or as if the ecosystem constituted a common brain.

An eleven-foot mother alligator may have a brain the size of a plum, but her huge tail is part of a nervous system that connects her to the ecosystem's radar system—where the word *system* is a basic denotation of the complexity of strategies among variations that border on the unfathomable. One result: incredibly complex forepaws, which create a deep and artful architectural structure that is the cultural equivalent of our skyscrapers—the wetlands "alligator hole." I have stood in one, tolerated by the mother and her young as long as my movements were respectful and nonaggressive. Here, the intelligence of the alligator-plus-ecosystem is commensurate with our own as a species, with her ecosystem an extension of her brainpower. Now imagine a human caged in a zoo—can we imagine it capable of producing the skyscraper?

In the same way, I have stood in the midst of two competing centers of the Kabbalah in Jerusalem: the university-educated descendants of the great historian of the Kabbalah, Gershom Scholem, on the one hand, and the followers of mystical rabbis on the other. I was welcomed into each circle, as long as I appeared respectful. I have spent many hours at Scholem's dining table as a guest of his widow, pouring over his marginal notes on kabbalistic texts he rediscovered. I have attended numerous mystical ceremonies and study groups in Jerusalem's "Old City," where psalms as well as the *Zohar* were chanted in the most heartbreaking melodies, as if they were lullabies sung by a mother to her slaughtered child. (The biblical figure of Rachel becomes just such an archetype in the Kabbalah. As she weeps in her exile, she represents the yearning for union of the Shekhinah, a female aspect and consort of the Creator.)

Each of these two worlds seemed in their own exile to me; each was cut off from the "way out of time" that the natural world can provide, either in the dream power and sexual poetry of the *Zohar*'s author or the frontier ecology beyond the university's walls. The birds that are "in exile" at Parrot Jungle would be altogether different in their natural home. We have taken away the foundation of their native intelligence, including the ability to build their own shelters, provide for themselves and their young, thrive—and, even more significantly, evolve. For the vast array of parrot species are all the result of "parrot exploration" of their ecosystems while reflecting on our own solitary status as a monospecies.

Exiled ourselves within human culture, our eyes are trained to see individuals or groups of individual species—not to "see" the ecosystem, as did the nervous systems of our parental species of primates in a rain forest. Since we have no intelligence yet of what our original *Homo sapiens* ecosystem was, we must grow new eyes— in the cultural sense—in order to find a new way to see ourselves in the evolutionary time of a creative ecosystem (that is, an ecosystem in which a diversity of new species continues to be created). Without these new eyes, we are blind to our natural significance— and this is just what a Kabbalist would describe as heartbreaking.

The Kabbalist, however, would couch it in terms of cosmic significance, for the complexity of the natural world was largely terra incognita to the civilized world until very recently.

The Kabbalist brings new eyes to the world, eyes developed from reading behind, beneath, above, and beyond the text and commentary of the Bible. The Kabbalist reader sees the text of the Bible as if in literal cages—a cause of poignant heartbreak and a desire to set it free. Recall, however, that the cages are not symbolic of cruelty but rather of human ignorance of the cosmic (or natural) world. For the Kabbalist, the cosmic world that includes heaven and eternity is a natural whole: the "upper world" includes angels and demons because they are projections of our inner world.

For access to the kabbalistic cosmos, heartbreak is central and essential. No matter how much intellectual study is involved, the reader cannot understand the text unless he or she has offered his heart to be broken on the altar of poetry. Not just any poetry, but prayer, which is founded on the humility of heartbreak just like the African-American tradition of the blues. Of course, the blues often travel a long way from sadness, for they require the transformation of heartbreak into a triumph of musical and poetic art. In the same way, kabbalistic prayer often reaches the realm of the ecstatic, incorporating all the poetic and magical techniques it can find to produce a higher art.

Since heartbreak cannot be acquired from conventional learning, how is it earned by the Kabbalist? If we ask the same question of the authentic blues or jazz musician, the answer is not simply "experience" but the experience of the African-American tradition, which is potentially available to European and other cultures in the same manner that the Jewish Bible is available to any reader, including but not exclusive to Christianity. This is why—and how—the Kabbalah reached the Christian world in the Renaissance and was translated into Christian forms that illuminated but never rivaled the literary core of the *Zohar*.

How is heartbreak acquired from tradition, especially a tradition of reading? By the inner exploration of loss. And by the connection to personal loss, which begins for all of us in childhood in the family romance that will turn our parents into fallen gods, if we are allowed to mature properly. In other words, it must be personal. Some will say that it should instead be social, that from our own disappointments we should be able to identify with the survivors of slavery or genocide. Or, more specifically, as those who have lived in the time of the Holocaust, we should more deeply appreciate a religion and liturgy forged in the catastrophic loss of Temple and homeland in ancient times.

To this, the Kabbalist answers, "No, the loss must be made personal. This is done through rigorous self-examination and soul-searching. Only then can a broken heart be brought to bear on the great text of the *Zohar*." I have noticed many sensitive colleagues read translations of the *Zohar* stone-faced, only to be dismayed by their incomprehension. This should be easy to picture for any American; just imagine our parents' (or grandparents') first recoil from Chuck Berry or Jimi Hendrix, not to mention Howlin' Wolf, Bessie Smith, or Blind Willie McTell—true blues sages. More exactly, imagine trying to explain the blues to an audience made up of Daughters of the American Revolution (as formerly constituted). "You have to *feel* it," you might say. In the Kabbalah, you also have to feel how the utter humiliation of humanity's most eminent scholars and sages can be transformed into the interpretive, poetic narrative of the *Zohar*, perhaps the most personal text of great literature we know.

Some will disagree. They may claim that it is relatively easy for the common man or woman to apply the Kabbalah to their lives and experience uplift. Perhaps more than uplift—success! What could be of higher value than success? Even though the Kabbalah counsels failure, brokenheartedness, the merchants of uplift need simply remove the old label and replace it with one that reads "Success."

Still others will claim that serious years of study and high academic degrees are required. These are the types of academics who claim that they can feel the pain of the blues (or the Kabbalah) more fruitfully than anyone else, so they must guard against the blues blindly reaching the "untutored ear." Another type of success is being defended here, the intellectual kind. But it is a temporary success like the others, even though it is one of scholarship. It is focused on enshrining the present and past to the extent that they exclude the future.

Building on the prophets of the Bible, the Kabbalah teaches

that a need for openness, for being brokenhearted, parallels our dreamlife, in which the soul may leave, ascend, and acknowledge the world beyond time. From that vantage, the present is the past. If we are in exile from our present, the success we have had there is less significant than the vision of the future in which we live.

6

Beyond commentary, the *Zohar* asks of the Bible: Who is the translator of its divine author? Since the *Zohar* is in one sense an interpretation of the Bible, the loss the reader feels first is one of authorship—of close connection to the divine voice at Mount Sinai. In order to get closer to that original voice, the reader must admit that the Torah itself is a translation; in it, the Creator has translated his message into limited human stories and other genres. We must find a way through the text to an echo of the divine voice itself—or if not the voice, at least the intention.

I will now add a modern corollary: it has recently become possible to feel the presence of the actual authors who wrote the Bible, such as the crucial writers "J" and "S" who wrote at the Solomonic court in the tenth century, B.C. A new type of translation has evolved in which these authors may reacquire their original identity so that we can come closer to their words. Did they consider themselves translators of the divine voice or as authors in their own right? All the evidence points to the latter conclusion, which also clarifies how the same fertile ambiguity gave rise to a renaissance for Moses de Leon and other Kabbalists in the twelfth to sixteenth centuries. By entering into this complexity on my own, my personal intention to turn the sexual loss and broken heart of various periods in my life into a collaboration with dreamers focused upon the future was realized.

Although the myths and dreams of the Kabbalah are known today to constitute a type of metaphysics, they are usually presented in neutered form. The Kabbalah, however, reveals that sex is messianic, future-oriented, and that it is a yearning for unity and for the body of the mother. The messianic desire for the end of time is equal to returning to the mother's body—the body of the Shekhinah, formerly taboo like our mother's, but now through her we can be reborn into the messianic age and out of exile, a place beyond time where the cosmos is in balance and we are not in danger of eating her (as in the biting fantasies of infants) or being eaten. That longing for unity is also why the Shekhinah receives the prayer that she be able to unite with the Creator—in other words, it is as if we are praying to make ourselves be born, both in retrospect and in a future.

The poignant aspect of this yearning is the catastrophe of our present. For the Kabbalist, it was not simply the fact of exile but the physically exposed position, subject to the hatred of being the outsider. Moses de Leon, for one, turned being outside into a virtue—just as I had longed to do in my narcissistic teens, finding myself locked out of the love I took to be original. Like a Kabbalist, I would learn to understand that sex was no simple matter in the natural scheme of things. I would need to study the psychology of the soul, of our inner lives. Such a serious attitude toward sex and psychology has only recently been extended from psycho-analysis to the entire living cosmos by the frontier ecology I have described. Sex, in this natural sense, means evolution and sexual prehistory, our origins, and psychology means the anxiety or stress that exists at each level of the ecosystem, right down to the bacteria underground.

But the soul also needs to sublimate sexuality, since the soul transcends mortality. The equivalent in the natural world becomes the species' drive to evolve. Sexuality is elevated into leaving our body. When we evolved into *Homo sapiens,* we entered a "perfected" body, with no memory of previous life. Yet the need and desire for sex is still as strong, if not stronger, even as the act of intercourse becomes our model for the supreme form of uniting our interior life and the future. In other words, the Kabbalah sexualized the soul long before our current scientific attempts.

One indication of the sexualized soul is the Kabbalah's concern with control of ejaculation. There was great fear in losing control over this life-giving power. Sexual intercourse had to be performed within a conscious framework that honored its cosmic significance. But the most dangerous time was when dreaming, which could lead to nocturnal emission. How could a man control this and overcome the danger? How could a woman control her own erotic dreams of becoming inseminated? The creative answer is in the *Zohar.* It is a matter of learning to see the beautiful disguises of dreams and words, and to see through them to the original voices in the Garden of Eden.

7

In this opening section, as in the closing one that follows my translations, I attempt to express **the reason for disguise** and the effect it has on people who are searching for a synthesis of inner knowledge with outward facts. The central metaphor of the Kabbalah itself is that the core of the Bible presents a beautiful disguise, right down to each single letter of its alphabet. A great deal of kabbalistic theory is busy justifying the necessity for this disguise.

I began to see the *Zohar*'s own disguise in terms of a critique of memory. Unlike approaching the memory and asking directly "What happened and when?", the Kabbalah knows that there is a subconscious mind, an interior world beneath conscious memory, and that it can only be approached indirectly. The method that Kabbalists developed for asking the cosmic questions was rather like reformulating them into a dream, as I have suggested—and then proceeding to "read" or resolve the dream.

My personal dream of cosmic questions turned out to be a nightmare in which I was about to die. So imagine the warmth I felt toward a fly upon waking from this nightmare. In the nightmare I was trapped by forces I could not control, forces alien to me, alien as death. The fly, on the other hand, was a fellow in life. He, or she, was shaped by the same forces as I was, forces that I sense are parental and not alien: sexuality, a body with eyes and appendages for mobility, a desire to eat and mate—and to explore. This fly was exploring me, in its way, as I was exploring it for signs of my being at home, here, in the world, and not in alien death.

Instead of an alien spirit, the fly represented my body without its human identity. The Kabbalah reveals the necessity to lose this identity—in the reading of the *Zohar,* for instance—and then to be restored by finding our way back. Reading becomes an allegory for the soul leaving the body and finding its way back during the night. We ourselves are that mortal text, made awake even under the exploring feet of a miraculously constructed and innocent fly—as innocent as the soul.

Studying the fly can teach us about the soul's exile in ways parallel to the *Zohar.* The fly reveals our own exile in nature, for it has a place in its natural ecosystem while we live in a world of cultural artifice, far from our natural origin. As the *Zohar* helps us read our way back to the Garden of Eden, evolutionary ecology teaches us to lift the garment of the landscapes of our own making—cities as well as countryside—and to read back to an original ecosystem. The way back is found as we learn to return each species, through its evolutionary history and genetic prehistory, to its proper home. The fly or any innocent living thing can act as a guide to see through the world's text to our original home: not a simplistic Garden of Eden but the place of our evolution in natural and sexual balance—a place every bit as complex as the *Zohar* imagines it.

The *Zohar*'s projection of the interior world of psychological exile into a vision of the future is one in which time is stopped but space is expanded. This fits in well with the scientific realm we might call ecological mind, where time is expanded—back through prehistory—while space is contracted, purged of spirits. Yet they are there—angels and demons as the *Zohar* relates—in the form of other species. If the present is seen as the past, as in prophecy, as already taking its place in memory, then we can be freer about imagining the future. If we can look back from a future that is like the "next life," one in which we have evolved, then we are already imagining other species as if they were angels or demons. My fly will have become an angel, for demons are the result of neglect and disease; we can see them now under microscopes as viruses and pathogens, or even as human despoilers.

We can also imagine that it is our soul reading the *Zohar*, full of joy to know it will be released. After all, it is our interior life projected into the act of reading, and it yearns to be outside of time, to be an immortal observer like our soul, if even for just a few hours of the night. In the later tradition of the Kabbalah that followed the *Zohar*, it was Abulafia and then Luria (the *Ari*, or "lion," of intellect) who represented this wish to be an outside observer in terms of knowing oneself.

8

As if it were a story by Kafka or Singer in a popular literary mag-
azine, the reader need not comprehend at first but rather experience
the cosmic background—in which the narrative may move from
our world to others, or a soul may leave its body during a dream.
The *Zohar* also demands the curiosity to discover the body beneath
the garment of its own text. This body is what I call the literary
core of the Kabbalah. It is a complex collage of myth, metaphor,
and narrative that seems to expect a knowledge of sources that few
have acquired.

It is up to the translator, then—a kabbalistic translator—to
find an imaginative form and context for the literary core. A literal
translation renders only the garment, while narrative selections
miss the complexity of form. Either of these types of translation
make the reader dependent on footnotes (rather than free to ignore
them), and this distorts the standard editions of the *Zohar*, which are
published in multiple volumes that disdain footnotes. Instead of
the labor of context, the Kabbalah begs for more kabbalistic texts,
not footnotes. The original *Zohar* is expanded by the *Zohar Hadash*
(the *New Zohar*) as well as other framing texts. In the end, these multiple layers are what make the *Zohar* such a great work.

What if the translator were to become a Kabbalist and find a new form that suggests the literary complexity of the original. Henry James, the classic American novelist, has written that "the greater complexity, the superior truth, was all more or less present to me; only the question was, too dreadfully, how make it present to the reader?" In response, I have attempted a form of dream, a serial narrative, in which episodes are woven together by threads of similar intensity, focus, and bearing. As in a dream, borders are crossed, suggesting a narrative of the soul as it seeks to elude the "other side."

❧

The Notes section at the end of this book reveal the sources of the episodes in Part II of this book. These episodes are largely from the *Zohar* and its additional framing texts, but a few selections within some episodes are from other kabbalistic texts and from the Midrash, which is the tradition of commentary that preceded and influenced the Kabbalah. I have included examples that come close imaginatively to the *Zohar*. Generally, the Midrash demands a homiletic structure that is more limiting to the imagination than the Kabbalah—in fact, a good number of the selections in the many volumes of the Midrash consist of ancient sermons. Although there are surprising stories and parables to be found in these, as well as ironic levels of biblical interpretation (hermeneutics), a complex literary core is lacking in the Midrash. Nor does it generally contain the bold harmonics of a cosmology and the framing myth of the soul that make up the *Zohar*. The layerings of the *Zohar* are unlikely to have derived from sermons, and the tenuous scaffold of biblical commentary functions almost like rhyme in a lyric poem: a spur to inventive twists and turns—and to imaginative leaps.

"The words of Torah are sublime secrets," postulates the *Zohar*. In other words, the secrets need to be interpreted, first; and, being sublime, they also ask to be shaped by an art that risks wildness of vision.

9

When I was in Sunday School, our introduction to psychology was to distinguish the good angel from the bad angel. Essentially nothing has changed in our common culture, where the journalistic credo of getting both sides of the story is sophisticatedly translated into the damaged interior life versus the smooth exterior—in other words, you can't predict behavior just from the way a person acts. A seemingly friendly do-gooder might turn out to be the murderer. Yet even when our interior life tells us that the outward self might be an act, it also casts doubt on itself, for on the inside we may invite victimization. It is the complexity of this insight about our inner lives from modern psychology that is not yet reflected in the public culture, but it is this same complexity that is represented in the *Zohar* by the trials of the soul.

As with all great art, it is not necessarily the characters, myths, or stories that have charmed us, but the way the author has used them to put our exteriors to sleep and address our interior lives. That is why authorship is so critical, for it has taught us to trust ourselves as the authors of our own lives, to accept ambivalence and ambiguity as required for the creation of "stories within stories." That is why the *Zohar* can "invent" its own authorship to give us the messianic Shimon bar Yohai as someone who speaks directly to our interior life or soul, for bar Yohai represents a future when outer and inner worlds will be united, body and soul. He crosses the borders of worlds because he can internalize any ambiguity, any mystery or secret. What does he know that we don't? He knows that the entire cosmos is one system, stretching before us and beyond us. Once again, that is what evolutionary ecology is trying to express today by crossing the borders of physics, biology, and other fields. It wants to tell us our future by connecting the evolution of our bodies in the natural world to the development of our interior lives, which seek ways and vantage points outside of time.

The interior life is made into a science in the Kabbalah. In a similar way, evolutionary ecology wants to understand the ecosystems in which species can evolve into hundreds of millions of kinds, while humans, still so young in time, remain only one species, *Homo sapiens*. Here is also our inner desire to untangle origins: to get back to the Garden of Eden where we evolved.

For Moses de Leon, literal commentary and even the psychologically literal "feelings" of yearning in prayer and study are inadequate. Instead, a new yearning for union through a literary experience motivates the *Zohar*'s author. Ritual and meditation on the *Zohar* itself came later, but first came literary freedom unlocked by the trope of collaboration. It is not tradition and commentary that holds here but the sense of collaboration with the biblical authors, with contemporary kabbalistic companions, with the ancient rabbis of Shimon bar Yohai's circle, and with the lost, literal, physical reality of Adam and Eve, the first *Homo sapiens.*

10

When the great books of ancient Jewish and Christian tradition
are invoked—the Bible, the Talmud, the Midrash, the Apocrypha,
the Saints and Philosophers—why is the Kabbalah rarely mentioned? Some have complained the Kabbalah is too mystical, while
others have suggested it is too fantastic, too ecstatic, too disturb-
ing, too embarrassing. It's none of these things to an open-minded
reader, because the actual texts of the Kabbalah barely exist in
translation. The *Zohar's* original language, a literary invention of
Aramaic-ized Hebrew, is under discussion among scholars, but
they are still sorting out issues of authorship: who wrote it, who
erased the authors, and the *why* behind these questions.

Instead of great books, then, the Kabbalah has been represented to the general reader as a compendium of codes, rituals, and
myths. These compendiums are accompanied by explanations not
of the texts themselves but of their secondary adjuncts—the
codes of numerology or the rituals of meditation, for example. In
recent years, many books that purport to explain the Kabbalah in
this manner have attempted to satisfy the popular interest in meditation and mysticism, but in the end these attempts are doomed,
for they have no vision of the Kabbalah's art. When the texts are

read by scholars, they are often misread. Scholars look for the light the texts throw on these systems and codes instead of looking for their own intrinsic value as great literature.

Let us come back to the *why:* Why must the *Zohar* remain such an "outside" work when its art is so contemporary? I believe the answer is that our culture has not yet found the vision of the future that is required. But I feel confident that vision is here, in frontier ecology, and that it is just a matter of time before culture as we now know it will be dazzled and changed by a new contact with the natural world, from which it is now insulated. Soon enough, the *Zohar* and its offshoots will tip the balance of Western culture and art more to what lies outside.

Part II

NEW TRANSLATIONS OF THE KABBALAH

DREAMS OF BEING EATEN ALIVE

Adam entered blithely, hardly knowing it was the ancient serpent, a silent, screaming temptation. His desire rose to her siren; he lowered himself to the strumpet.

❧❦❧

Adam did not realize he had never before seen her. Thinking she was a mate—she had the soft voice of Eve—he was not careful. She appeared as a creation for him, a spirit visiting him in sleep.

❧❦❧

Meanwhile, he avoided intercourse with Eve. In his sleep, however, he continued to be visited by female spirits, and union with them bore ghosts and demons.

⟨❧⟩

One night, his undergarment wet, Adam removed it and reentered his bed—suddenly a bed of water, a trap. When Eve appeared she removed his covers. Distressed—she was fully dressed—he dared not think of his own nakedness. Frozen by embarrassment, he sunk deeply down, covering himself again to the neck.

She was exquisitely clothed, as if an actress in the first drama. He was beguiled by memory come to life, a light slap in the face, a first kiss. She spoke curvaceously, her mouth a newly discovered fruit. His thought became froth there, leaving him speechless, lip-reading. Then a fear of deafness followed; he could feel his hairline recede, crawling up his skull. He was confined in a place that felt well-like (he whose place had been everywhere) and he was unmanned.

Yet unbroken, wild, his yearning cut a swath to her—out and away from a fear to be breathing his last, to be turning to dust.

Observe a secret beyond secrets: it erupts from a blazing noon in Adam's mind, exudes from the wine dregs Isaac would drink—from both, a mottled fungus appears. Rose-red, it is all rose: male and female in one. As a flame, it unfolds in many directions of time, from Adam forward to Isaac.

On the other side of that noon, the male is called Samael, his mate a part of him, within. On the pure side it is the same, a reflection: the male and female locked in embrace. Samael's female is named Serpent, siren woman. At the end of all flesh she is known to lie in waiting, on a body's last day she is waiting to be entered. Together, they are the limits of contempt locked in one embrace: the male spirit is subtle, the female distracted in many directions, lying on many paths—but locked to the male in spirit.

See it clearly: the couple were one, as if fastened to the same rock in an ancient fresco—and the rock had been through a weathering process, leaving it smooth-looking, the movement of their coupling almost imperceptible. He advanced his hands over her body slowly, as if anointing her.

In their movement, they seemed under a mushroom-colored coverlet, their limbs braided together.

They appeared—new wine in old bottles—a fermenting color. As their entwined figures wobbled, a shuddering wave appeared to flow over them.

As if the organ of the brain could be imagined to conceive, a vine rises from the grave bed: its flowers the unspoken words, a language of Samael's spirits, accusing. The entire aspect appears designed by a man absorbed—but without hands, embracing it in his mind. Meanwhile, a pain builds in Adam that Isaac feels as he sleeps, a stimulation, a hemorrhaging: he wanted to wake, to be there—to stop it and announce his presence, master of this shame.

At the climax, the spirit was released and Adam saw Isaac's offspring, two sons embracing in struggle. There, in his own grave—Adam could see into time, past the flowers, beyond the lichen, as if a womb had opened and contained all the words that would be spoken.

Isaac's old bones did not look as if they could hold up a father of young children and, similarly, Rebecca appeared to have traveled too far down nature's path to bear children. When pregnant seven months, she wished that the curse of childlessness had not been withdrawn. The pain was appalling: the twin sons had begun their life's-worth of dueling—to the death, it would seem. Samael worked through Esau, who would have cut off Jacob in his mother's womb.

Now return: Adam and Eve are still in Paradise when Samael, with a little boy in tow, accosts Eve. "Would you mind merely keeping an eye on my son?" he asks her. "I will soon return." Eve agrees.

Returning from a walk in Paradise, Adam follows the piercing squeals of the child back to Eve.

"It is Samael's," she tells a vexed Adam. His anxiety increases along with the screams of the little one, which grow unbearably violent. Beside himself, Adam delivers a blow that kills the youngster then and there. Yet its body continues to wail at a fever pitch, monstrous groans that do not stop when Adam cuts the corpse into bits.

Then Adam cooked the pieces of flesh and bone that remained, to wipe out this fiend. Together with Eve, he ate all that was left. They had hardly finished when Samael called for his son. Denying any knowledge of his son, the culprits were protesting their innocence when suddenly a louder voice cried out from within their stomachs to silence them: it was the dead boy's voice, come straight from their hearts, his words directed to Samael.

"Leave me, now that I've pierced the hearts of both Adam and Eve. I remain in their hearts forever, and in their children's hearts, their children's children—until the last generation I abide here."

⬥

Up and down Lilith went until she reached the baby-faced cherubs. She would not budge from them, longing to assume their shape, to never leave. The divine one blessed us in wresting her away, forcing her down below. Then he created Adam and his partner, and when Lilith saw Eve attached to Adam's back—their beauty reflecting perfection— she flew up again, longing to behold the baby faces.

Yet the celestial gatekeepers blocked her, and the divine one in his blessing scolded, casting her down toward the bottom of the sea. She was living there until the day of Adam and Eve's contempt.

At that time, the divine one in his blessing brought her up from the sea, to rule over the baby faces of mankind: for their father's sin they are already sentenced. Pacing the earth back and forth, she finds the place of the Garden, and there at the gates she sees the guardian cherubs—and then the blazing sword. There she abides, near the essence of her origin.

When Cain is born, Lilith wanted to (but could not) attach herself to him, so she turned to him to accept his penetration, bearing demons and spirits. Adam himself ejaculated with female spirits for a hundred and thirty years, when Naamah was born. She is the one who strays about at night, agitating the sleeping sons of men until they are stained with their own semen.

A child was born of Isaac's dream and nocturnal emission. Rebecca did not know of it. The secret consumed Isaac; he couldn't sleep. Finally, he planned to tell Rebecca at a dinner arranged for themselves in private (he ordered a stew prepared).

"What is this dinner for?" she asked.

"I have a story to share," he answered. "A tale long growing in my dreams, until now it consumes me."

"A woman approached as I was reading the Garden story in the scroll. I was thinking of the serpent, his intelligence, how much like a woman—in the dream. 'Subtle,' I was thinking, and then the woman appeared. As if she had been in the corner all along, too shy to speak, I thought. Yet she spoke freely, smooth-tongued. 'You, scrollworm,' she whispered, 'I can read your mind. You were meditating on Samael, and I was drawn to you.'

"I found her irresistible. She emptied my mind by fascination, and then took over. I thought: For the first time I know what it feels like to be a woman. And then I began to laugh, uncontrollably, and she joined in. 'You see,' she said, 'I read your thoughts, with no help from philosophy.'

"I became very nervous; it seemed I was trapped in a tent during a long rain. I looked down and my knuckles were white as they gripped the scroll handles. I became dizzy, the scene blurred and then I saw that I gripped her arms, was staring into her face—in place of the scroll. Running through the middle of her forehead—similarly, her chin—a startling dimple, as if it were the crease between the pages of an opened prayer book. Her face was luminescent, a halo itself for the defining furrow in the middle, the dimple.

"And then—rain gone—and in an instant I was overexposed in desert sun. In the grip of this intense moment, I was blind with dread.

"Night after night, she grew familiar to me. All her features were exaggerated in some way: eyes and bosom large; exquisitely small nose; long, long fingers. I was joined with her, slowly and all of a sudden—I was falling from a great height, so that one can tell it only by a sinking feeling inside, spirit sucked out in the cold damp air.

"Then one night, expecting her to appear—I didn't bother even to read further in the scroll—a small girl came crawling on all fours toward me. I stared at this wonder, saw that she was in all ways like her mother, except without exaggerations. A model of perfection. Thereupon you came in, Rebecca, your hand went to your mouth and as the child saw you, she screamed, would not stop. You did not ask who or from where the girl came. You began to wheeze, with great groans in rhythm with each louder shriek of the baby girl, until both of you were red-faced. Finally, you pushed me with a strange strength, lifted up the infant, and flung her through the open window.

"In the courtyard she continued the screeching; you went down, returned with her, placed her on the kitchen table and with the carver lopped off her limbs and sawed through the neck. Yet the head still wailed, the limbs flailing. All the while I'm frozen in disbelief, in fear of you; I can't move. You gather up the pieces, force them into a pot, light the fire, boil them. A calm comes over you as you cook, adding vegetables and spices. 'Cut up these vegetables,' you say and I do.

"'Set the table,' you command and I fulfill the order. As we were eating we drank the new wine."

At this very moment Isaac looked down at his meal and the wineglass beside it, then at Rebecca. She continued eating, unfazed by all he was telling.

"I told you it was not good to practice union while drunk with the new wine," she said momentarily. "You reproach yourself in your dreams but I have seen the results; I cannot hide it. I find your dried seed in the sheets in the morning. If you must have wine—no more than a glass."

As Rebecca put down her fork her brows were knit. "But, Isaac, this is dangerous. You should not think of it. Put it out of your mind."

Then she gasped. "It was the new wine that made us drunk that night: this same bright red wine we are drinking." And she flung her glass to the floor.

Someone knocked. Isaac turned as white as he had imagined himself in the dream. Rebecca answered the door, found a blind man, hand cupped to his mouth in a repeated gesture, as if feeding himself. Food? Was it food he wanted? He made a biting gesture, repeatedly. She brought food and he caressed a chicken bone with his hand, did not eat.

A choking scream. "Isaac, what happened?" she exclaimed, returning to find him sprawled on the couch. "The child, the child," he murmured. "Tell him to go. Shut the door in his face, hurry."

Then he explained: "It was in my dreams too. The voice of the girl tore at my heart like a daughter; I couldn't ignore it—abandoned like my own daughter. A voice from the stew kept speaking, in a low murmur: 'I have lost my heart and you will lose yours. To the end of days, the end of all flesh, all living hearts must be broken—a piece broken off and eaten, sticking in your throat.'

"I woke up, couldn't fall back asleep, could not even swallow. That is why you heard me many times going out for water."

Rebecca groaned and clung to Isaac, these old ones twined together as ancient vines.

<hr>

"You looked forward to the death of Adam, to make his wife your bride. I make you enemy to woman, enmity bound between your seed and hers." And the angels were made the bearers of this sentence. They came down from heaven to chop off his hands, his feet. So wild was his pain, screams of torment were heard from one end of the world to the other.

⟨≈≋≋≋≋⟩

Soon Rebecca was noticeably ready, and then gave birth to twins. Isaac was almost blind, so Rebecca read to him. Then, in bed once again, they clung together in union.

Jacob climbed down from his crib and crawled toward his parents' bedroom, where he heard their whispers. Closer, he heard his mother's whimpers coming from the bed; then he saw his father above her, thrashing. He sunk back on his knees, transfixed with fear.

A low moaning now came from his mother. Jacob pulled in his head, touching his forehead to the floor. He heard the wheezing and pummeling of his father grow louder, the bed creaking as though it would break.

What had his mother done to deserve this? Why did she not cry out for help? She began to gasp for breath; Jacob feared for his life. His father would beat him also, and for having spent time at her breast he would be killed. He tried to look away, raised his elbows over his head, then buried his face in the matted carpet, his hands clasped tightly together.

Now his mother's breath came in little shouts. Soon she would be dead, he thought. Jacob wanted to scream, to howl, but he was afraid his father would murder him on the spot. He tried to back out of the room, though his legs did not want to move, as if locked, and as if his head was joined to the floor.

How could such force be left in the frail body of his father? Jacob's body trembled as he heard the sudden love cries of his mother, warm, high-pitched, as if they were his own crying out in his sleep. He burst into great sobs, drowning out his parents' dying murmurs. They jumped from the bed as if the clumsy vines of their exhausted embrace were chopped asunder.

⟡

When Jacob grew into a boy, his father Isaac heard a command that his meek son Jacob be married to a Canaanite priestess. It came in a low voice that made Isaac shiver—so thoroughly intimate with him. It was as if the voice were within, his own, his father's. Then he identified it in panic: the disembodied, guttural voice from the stew.

Jacob followed a strange song out into the fields. He told his father the story of this voice. Fearing it was the same siren song, a shaken Issac sent his son to fetch his older brothers, who were pasturing the flocks near Dothan.

On his way, Jacob felt the singer pursuing, as a magnet is drawn to the truth. The descant trailed him; he went hurriedly, stumbling over a stone here and there, as if lost in listening. So clear the air became, he imagined the earth smell of her hair.

⟡

Dressed up like a fancy whore, she waits gaudily for men drawn to her, standing by crossroads and highway corners. As a man accosts her, she hugs him with fondling kisses, then mixes her cheap wine with venom for him. Now he has drunk and forgotten his journey in order to pursue her. She sees he has left the way of truth to come with her and now removes the showy mask and costume: she dissolves the disguises this man has swallowed.

Here is the masquerade by which mankind is seduced: her hair is long, red like a lily, her face white and pink; six pendants hang at her ears; her bed is made of Egyptian flax; all the ornaments of the East encircle her neck; her mouth is shaped like a tiny door, beautified with cosmetic; her tongue is sharp like a sword, her words smooth as oil, her lips beautiful, dripping lily-red, sweetened with all the sweetnesses in the world; she is dressed in purple, cloaked in thirty-nine items of finery.

So the man has followed her, consumed her cup of wine, and entered her wanton arms, fully enchanted with her. What does she do? While he sleeps in her bed she goes up to heaven to accuse him. Warrant in hand, she comes down to watch the man awake. He is eager to fondle her familiarly, but as she removes her clothes, out steps a ferocious warrior in an armor of blazing fire: a vision of dread that seizes body and soul. Full of gaping eyes, this other holds a sharpened sword with drops of venom suspended and dripping from it. He kills the man, throws him into the abysmal pit.

He was in a trance. His head seemed to levitate above his body as she came from behind, so that he backed into her, or fell backward. The notes of her syllables entered in one ear and exited the other in perfect order. His hands felt silky against her smooth skin, yet he could not tell where she was, beneath or behind, his hands groping along bald air.

He heard something—deep sobs, or was it cackling? Where was he? Yes, a cackling, and in his hands, hair.

And he began to understand: she was grunting in a vernacular he had learned as a child and almost forgotten, barely knew, a rural accent that struck a deep chord in him: a childhood and its innocent dreams lost. She was the instrument of it, mocking human brevity in hoarse lullabies of death.

In his arms he held a skeleton. The hair in his hands was soft and greasy as worms: she had dissolved. His eyes reopened; he saw the house he was truly within; a pit opened within him, a deflowered garden. He was mated to her, found himself standing in bile—in a liquid, pulsing grave. Then his mind began to levitate, his body an empty bag in her arms. He found himself above ground, on the lip of the pit. The sun shone, and then a shadow fell over him. He turned to face—her face again, restored in a man's body. "You are a two-faced Jacob," the other was saying. "You have sent me up into the moonlight from below."

Her male countenance was deformed by fury; all face was lost. Yet what did he do, what offense? The virile one flew at Jacob with a weight as if dropped from heaven. He rose quickly like a dead actor from the stage, found grim strength in himself. His body appeared to mimic the other's, as if lip-reading with all his limbs. They grappled evenly for a long time, back and forth. From a distance they seemed a single otherworldly figure acting out the telling of a portentous war.

The virile one spewed impenetrable sounds of labor as Jacob opposed him in a standoff, matching his every maneuver. Neither could the virile one overpower Jacob, nor overcome his own indignation at the light of day.

***

He saw all through the rich facade of her house, withdrew himself after entering. Samael, her mate, was shamed, came down to pin him there, but he could not dim the perception's power.

***

First, it happened: "My father," Isaac asked Abraham....Meanwhile, Samael approached the patriarch Abraham, chastising him: "Old man, what are you doing? Are you crazy? How can you go off to kill a son with whom you were blessed when a hundred years old?"

"I will go even this far," said Abraham.

"But if He puts before you an even greater test, how much can you stand?" asked Samael.

"I will go even farther," he said.

"Tomorrow he will tell you, 'You are a murderer, a guilty man.'"

"I will be content," he answered.

Getting nowhere with Abraham, Samael turned to Isaac: "A mournful mother's son you are. He goes off to kill you."

"I accept my fate," he answered.

"So all the superior tunics your mother made for you will become the despised Ishmael's, as a reward?"

⟨⁓⟩

Samael rode his mate, Lilith, through the night; he on her serpentine back, she curling her tail around him, holding him firmly there. In his ear she curled her tongue, whispering to him the happiness she felt: their son had found his way to the heart of the human.

"Yet there is something I must tell you," Samael

said later to Lilith. "The boy will never be seen again." Lilith was astonished, wounded; it had not occurred to her that Samael could give up their son forever. She wailed, legs coiling around Samael as if to strangle him. "This you did for the love of Eve. For my part, I will entertain every man I might, until the last man at time's end—where my boy waits for me, in him."

⚜

Now Sarah took Isaac into her bed, with caresses and soothings, binding him to the promises of devotion she desired, until it was morning. Then Sarah came out to the road where Abraham and Isaac were preparing to leave, walking beside them when they mounted.

"Return to the tent," they ordered her. Hearing these words come also from her son Isaac hurt Sarah deeply; then Abraham wept with her, and then Isaac, too, making a great weeping—to which the wails of the servants who went with them were piercingly added. Now Sarah grasped hold of Isaac, pulling him toward her, her arms wrapping around him.

"Who is it who knows if I will ever see you again?" Sarah sobbed. "Who can tell me this is not the last day?"

From the *Zohar*

LEAVING
THE BODY

When the soul leaves the body, it first transmits an account of its actions in life, and this is prepared together with the body. This event ensues from the arrival of Judgment Day, when the book of records opens and the accusers emerge. The snake also is brought forward, prepared to bite into the body, the limbs terrified and trembling.

After the soul has been severed from the body, it continues its journey, its path unknown, the destination unknown. It is a trembling day. Extricated, the soul drifts aimlessly, unable to ascend until the body is buried. Best to keep that day always in mind, the one in which you will be lowered into the ground to decompose and the soul abandons your body.

When that day is kept in mind the heartbreak can

be borne. Remember that the evil instinct craves abandonment to wine and revelry in order to join the celebration. But when the spirit is heartbroken, evil won't stay; it must withdraw. Always remember your deathday, keep heartbreak in your mind—and your body will be free of it.

Zohar 1:201b–202a

He raises his eyes and sees the angel of death standing in front of him with sword unsheathed in his hand: the man's jailer, torturer, and executioner. There is nothing more difficult for the soul than to separate from the body. No man dies before he sees the divine mother—and because of its deep yearning for her [the Shekinah] the soul departs in order to greet her. Once it has departed, what determines which soul can cleave to her, be received within her? These things have been explained.

When the soul has departed from the body and the body is bereft of a spirit, it is forbidden to leave the body unburied. Consider the possibility that, according to the divine, this man was sentenced to death in order to involve him in another transmigration immediately, on that very day, and for his own good. While the body remains unburied the soul cannot come into the presence of the divine or enter a different body in a transmigration, for the soul is unable to acquire another body until the first is buried. It is like a man whose wife has died. It is not right for him to marry another before he has buried the first.

Zohar 3:88a—88b

The ladder symbolizes the stairway, set on the altar of earth. Recall: the odor of the sacrifices ascended to heaven. Recollect: the High Priests, ascending and descending the stairway.

A ladder symbolizes Sinai. And they stood at the bottom of it. And the mountain burned and smoked to the heart of heaven.

And Moses went up, and Moses came down from the mount.

Midrash Rabbah: Genesis 58

THE ANGEL OF
DEATH DANCING

One of the rabbis was on his way to visit the masters and learn. As he came to the house of Rav Shimon bar Yohai, a fiery curtain flashed before his eyes. Stunned, he said to himself: I will stay here, outside, and listen to a word from his mouth.

"Escape, beloved, fly as a gazelle," he heard someone exclaim. And then an explanation: "There is but one demand by Israel of the Divine, as Rav Shimon tells it. 'It is Israel's desire that neither should the Divine go away nor turn away, but rather that he fly away as a gazelle.' Why this?

"Rav Shimon elucidates: 'Only one creature in the world acts like the gazelle. As it runs away it goes slowly at first and turns its head back to watch the place it has left. Its head keeps turning back.' 'Likewise, master of the universe,' implores Israel, 'if we make you turn away from us, fly likewise as the gazelle, its head turning back to watch the place it has left.'"

Zohar 2:14a–15a

Rav Isaac wept, knowing his days were numbered. He turned to Rav Shimon and found him studying Torah. As Rav Shimon raised his eyes toward Rav Isaac, he saw the angel of death skipping and dancing in front of him. "Has the image of your father appeared to you today? When a man is about to leave this world, his father and his closest friends are there—this we have learned. The man sees them and knows them."

Rav Isaac fell into a trance. He sees his father. "How favored you are in this world," says the father, "as well as in the next. In the Garden of Eden, under the leaves of the tree of Life, a tree is planted that is sturdy in both worlds: it is Rav Shimon bar Yohai. Now you are held in his branches. My son, how favored you are."

"Father, please, what will happen to me there?"

"For days they were preparing your room, planning even that the windows remain open, receiving light from the four quarters of the world. Then I saw where you were, and happiness entered into more than my eyes. How favored you are—except that your son is still ignorant of Torah."

"Father, please, how long do I have in this world?"

"I am not allowed to say. Man is not to be told. However, when Rav Shimon's great feast arrives, and on the day his soul ascends, you will still be at his table."

As Rav Isaac awoke, he was smiling. His face shone. Rav Shimon saw it, this face. "Has some word been imparted to you?" he asked.

"Yes." And he told it, falling to his knees before Rav Shimon, his teacher.

It is said that from that day on, Rav Isaac took his son's hand and taught him Torah. He never left him behind. Concerning Rav Shimon, the angel of death remained behind.

Zohar 1:217b–218b

Traveling on his donkey with his companions, Rav Pinchas met two Arabs. "Do you know of any voices being heard in this field?" he asked them.

"About the past we cannot say. In our day, some bandits who held up travelers once crossed this field. When they met some Jews they were ready to attack. Then the voice of a donkey came over this field from a long distance away, braying twice, and the sound was followed by a bolt of fire that scorched them. The Jews were saved."

"Arabs, Arabs," he exclaimed, "you yourselves will be saved today from bandits. They are hiding out by the road, waiting for you."

Zohar 3:200b–202b

"How will we know where Rav Shimon is?" asked the companions.

"The master of my donkey's footsteps," he answered, "will guide his steps there." Without urging, the donkey turned off the road and continued for two miles, arriving there. He brayed three times. Dismounting, Rav Pinchas said: "We must prepare to receive an appearance of the Ancient of Days. He comes to meet us—long aspect and short aspect—in the form of Rav Shimon and his son."

Rav Shimon heard the donkey's braying. "Rouse yourselves," he said to his companions, "the voice of the donkey beneath a just man has been moved to greet us."

⁂

The animals who had seen their first wonder sang divine words as they lowed. Yet how much more authentic the song of this braying donkey, belonging to a just man who is more familiar with miracles.

"Friends, you may object. 'No donkey has ever done that in all creation,' you may say. Yet come and contemplate the ancient ass of Balaam the ungodly, who surmounted her master at every turn. Now, isn't the donkey of Rav Pinchas as fitting an actor? Remember, when Balaam's ass spoke, an angel hovered over her. Friends, the time has come to reveal it. Listen: the mouth of the ass was among the things created in the dusk on the eve of the Sabbath. Was it open from that moment, or did the divine one set requirements at that time — requiring a miracle? It was nothing like that. It is a mystery for scholars, those who can look past the giddiness of the heart. The 'mouth of the ass' — the female power of the ass in the upper world — embodied that ass and spoke from above her."

Remember: the Sabbath day arose over all others, and it was called "the mouth of the Lord." For a moment at dusk, on the eve of the Sabbath, the mouth ascendant over all can be heard.

They went out to meet Rav Pinchas. When he arrived, Rav Pinchas kissed Rav Shimon. "I have kissed the mouth of the Lord, sweet-smelling spices from his garden."

Happy in each other's company, they sat down. At that moment, all the birds that above them were giving shade flew off. Rav Shimon turned and roared after them, "Birds of heaven! Respect the grandeur of your Master, as it is here."

The birds froze in place.

"Tell them to keep to their journey," said Rav Pinchas to Rav Shimon. "They have no permission to come back."

"I know there is a miracle the divine wants us to see. 'Birds, birds, keep to your journey and tell whoever your master is, that his power is diminished. I have neutralized it until the Day of Judgment.'"

The birds scattered and were gone. Now the companions saw three trees nearby and their branches were spreading over them. In front of them, a stream began to flow. They were happy, all of them.

"The birds have gone through a great deal of distress," said Rav Pinchas. "We should not cause animals to be frightened. 'His tender mercies cover all his creation,' as it is written."

<hr/>

"Like a tree planted by a stream of water" is the one who studies. A tree has seven parts: roots, bark, pith, branches, leaves, flowers, and fruit." These amount to seventy in the tree of Life. Just so, words of Torah contain literal meaning, then a moral one, then imaginative allusions, numerical analogies, concealed mysteries, and unspeakable mysteries—transcendent, one after another, clean and unclean, permitted and forbidden. The tree branches out from here on all sides. A student of Torah shall be like a tree itself. If not, he will not master wisdom, not enter the branches.

Zohar Hadash, Va-yera, 26b

On this day Rav Shimon went outside and found the world dismal and gray, its light shut away. "Come, we'll see what the divine one may require," Rav Eleazar said to him.

On their way they found an angel in the form of a towering mountain, with thirty, fiery flames streaming from his mouth. "What are you doing?" Rav Shimon asked him.

"I am trying to destroy the world," the angel said.

"Thirty just men no longer endure in this generation."

Rav Shimon replied, "Please, return to the divine one and give him this message: 'Bar Yohai exists in the world.'"

The angel did so, saying, "Master of the universe, you have heard what Bar Yohai has asked of me."

"Go, destroy the world, and ignore Bar Yohai." Such was the divine response.

As Rav Shimon saw the angel approach, he said: "If you do not keep away from here, I will cancel your return to heaven and you will join the fallen angels. Go, and when you return to the divine presence, say that if not thirty just men, let twenty be enough. If not twenty, let ten be enough. If not ten, then two: myself and my son. And if not two, at least one, myself: 'The just man is the foundation of the world,' as it is written."

Just at that moment a voice burst out of heaven: "What happiness fills your measure, Rav Shimon. The divine makes a judgment in the upper world, and you invalidate it in the world below—as only a just man can."

⟨═✦═⟩

Rav Shimon was seated at the Lydda gate. His eyes rose to the shining sun—for its light was almost erased three times, and in each dimming, the colors green and black appeared on the sun.

"Follow me, my son," he said to Rav Eleazar. "A judgment has been rendered in the world above and we'll see what the divine one wishes me to know. A judgment made above is deferred for thirty days, giving the just man time to be told. As it is written: After revealing his secrets to his prophets, the divine one acts."

On their way they cross a vineyard and see there a snake gliding by, open-mouthed, scorching the earth in its path. Rav Shimon reached down for it, holding its head in his hands. The snake was calmed, closing its mouth, but Rav Shimon noticed its tongue was still moving. "Snake, snake," he said, "return to the primordial serpent and tell him that Rav Shimon bar Yohai exists in the world."

The snake put its head in a crevice in the earth.

Then they noticed that the sun was shining, the

dimness gone. "The world smells fresh and sweet," said Rav Shimon.

Zohar 3:15a

Rav Rechumi was old and blind when he was visited by Rav Pinchas at the sea of Galilee. "I have a reliable account that our companion, bar Yohai, possesses a jewel," the old one says. "I have seen it within me: a vision streaming with light like the sun uncovered and illuminating the world. Follow this jewel, for this is your hour."

Two birds were skimming over the water of the lake. "Birds, birds," Rav Pinchas called to them, "have you seen bar Yohai?"

"Birds, birds," he called, "search for him and come back to me." And they flew off.

He boarded a boat and crossed the lake. Before he had disembarked the birds returned, a message in the mouth of one. "Bar Yohai has left the cave," it read, "together with his son, Rav Eleazar."

Rav Pinchas went there and found him changed almost beyond recognition, his body covered in mold from the cave. Rav Pinchas wept and cried, "I am undone, to have seen you so."

"Your lot is a happy one to see me so," said Rav Shimon. "If you had not found me in this condition, I would not have attained wisdom."

Zohar 1:11a–11b

Rav Shimon bar Yohai had grown very weak. "A man lies on his deathbed," he said, "and his case is opened in the heavenly court. Some are ready to acquit him and emphasize his merits; some want to convict him, stressing his guilt. The case does not go as the defendant would wish. But the divine one, king over all, is beneficent: when a man is judged in such a trial he emerges favorably. And why? We who have studied the divine know that he is always moved toward acquittal, moved to forgiveness. When I ask that he judge my state, I expect to pass through the thirteen doors of mercy to the world to come, no one to stop me. The doorkeepers will step aside, prevented from checking my permission."

As Rav Shimon continued in conversation, his visitors struggled to see him: he was no longer there. They were amazed, stunned into silence; a deep dread fell over them. Then, as they sat there, the fragrance of myriad spices drifted over, until their courage came back and they began to see Rav Shimon again, talking. They saw nothing else, however, and no one with whom he was speaking. And then Rav Shimon asked them: "What did you see?"

"Nothing," said Rav Pinchas. "We were astounded that we could not see you at all, not for the longest time. When we saw you again, the spices of the Garden of Eden overcame us. We could see nothing else. Your voice was speaking, but with whom—we could not know."

"Mine were the only words you heard? None other?"

"None," they answered.

"You are not ready to enter the presence of the Ancient of Days," Rav Shimon continued. "Still, it is surprising how Rav Pinchas saw nothing, since I was facing him at that moment in the upper world, below my son, Rav Eliezer. Just now, I was sent for, and the place of the just was revealed to me—in the world to come. I chose my place and ascended there, along with three hundred just souls. Adam was above; he sat beside me and conversed. He asked that his true sin continue to be unfathomable in the world of ordinary men—except for what the Torah already tells of it."

Zohar Hadash, Bereshit, 18d–19a

Though death was brought into the world through Adam, he cannot be held responsible for the death of men. There came a time when he said to God: "I am not concerned about the death of corrupt ones, but I could not bear the devoted ones reproaching me, laying the blame for their death upon me. I beg you, make no mention of my guilt."

God promised to grant his wish. So, when a man is about to die, God appears to him, and asks that he put down in writing all his deeds throughout his life. God explains: "You are dying on account of your evil deeds." When this record is finished, God orders him to seal it with his seal. Now, these are the writings that God will bring out on the judgment day, as each man faces up to his deeds. So, as soon as life is extinct in a man, he is presented to Adam and accuses him of having caused his death. Now Adam can reject the charge: "I committed just one misdeed. Is there any among you, however devout, who has not been guilty of more than one?"

Midrash Rabbah: Genesis

THE POWER OF
LILITH TO
CONSUME A CHILD

When Lilith saw her—Eve was attached to Adam's
back—Eve's radiance in Eden resembled the world
above. Lilith stared at her perfect form, then shrank
from approaching Adam. She escaped from there,
hoping to rejoin the cherubim. But the gatekeepers
in heaven kept her out, and she was cast to the bottom of the sea.

There she lived, until Adam and his wife sinned.
Then Lilith was released from the sea by the divine
one, to take charge now of the "cherubim" of
mankind: the infants, the ones in particular who are
to be punished for the sins of their fathers. From one
end of the world to the other, she searches for
infants who are to be disciplined. She smiles at

them, and then kills them. When the moon is on the wane, she may be nearby.

Zohar 1:19b

The snake—who was the fallen angel, Samael—lay with Eve, his slime entering her, and thus she gave birth to Cain. All the world's corrupt ones, those in each generation, come from this origin, when demons and spirits were generated, and that is why they share attributes with them. That is why, too, spirits and demons are partly like humans in the lower world and partly like angels above.

Now one particular male demon, called Tubal-Cain, was brought into the world in Cain's wake. A certain female arrived with him, named Naamah; she is the one after whom humans stray. Through her, more demons come into the world, and these hover in the air, agents of intelligence for the others dwelling below in the spirit underworld.

Into the world Tubal-Cain introduced weapons of war. Naamah continues her derisive howl to this day, she and her minions. From beneath the breakers of the great sea, where she makes her home, she comes to humanity and ridicules it. She grows hot with desire from men that she encounters while they dream, holding them tight. Stimulating their desire until consummation, the seed they spill in the night makes her pregnant with other demons who will enter the world.

Soon, sons she mothers from mortal men enter the dreams of females, impregnating them until they bear more spirits. When born, these make their way to Lilith, and she raises them. Meanwhile, Lilith searches the world for human babies, and when they are found she clings to them, too—in order to smother them, and then to consume these human babies' spirits, to make them her own.

If a man is impure, then during intercourse he may also attract a spirit from the other, impure side of the world. She will arrive to ridicule the newborn child—and if she kills it she will consume the spirit, to become one with it.

You may object and point out that some of the infants she kills have their spirits taken by pure angels from above. In those cases, you may ask, why was she the one allowed to kill them? Because those men and women may have strayed but did not have any intention of being impure or defiled. Lilith's power may control the body, therefore, but not the spirit.

Zohar 3:76b–77a

THE NONHUMAN WORLD

Come now and watch. Much can be learned from even the plague. When the divine one allows a plague of leprosy to visit a house, and it rubs off from one onto the other, the plague will not leave the house—not even when the spirit of defilement is gone. Not, that is, until the house is completely torn down, the stones stripped from each other and the wood pulled apart. Then the place may be purified. So it is with a body, limbs, and bones.

Zohar 3:55b

"There are many who are ranged against you," the divine one says to Israel, "ready to accuse you. If

you are turned toward me, your strength and help,
you will be shielded when outside and safe inside, in
your houses. You will sleep in your beds while I
stand guard around them—as well as outside.
Come now, watch. As evil ones approach a man's
door, they look up and gaze upon Shaddai, my
name engraved on the doorpost mezuzah with filli-
gree crowns embellished over the letters. The name
shatters them all. They must turn and flee, in fear of
a just man's door."

Zohar 3:266a

And Jacob dreamed. So did Nebuchadnezzar. The
ladder suggests an image—the same letters as in
Nebuchadnezzar's image, the strength of a dragon.
Now Nebuchadnezzar had a great dragon which
swallowed up everything thrown to it. When the
king boasted of it, Daniel replied, "Give me a
chance, and I will weaken him." Given the chance,
what did Daniel do? He took straw, hid nails in it,

and threw it to the dragon, and the nails lacerated his bowels.

Midrash Rabbah: Genesis 58

"He causes the grass to grow" suggests the six hundred million angels, even though they came into being on the second day of Creation. They are made of fire, and yet they are also grass. How? Like grass, they grow and are cut down every day, and then they spring up again as at first.

Zohar 3:217a

Seven heavens are above us. Stars, planets, and messengers exist in each of them. Each contains angels assembled like chariots, awaiting their Master's service. The chariots and messengers are different in each heaven: some have six wings, some four; some with four faces, others with two, and some with just one face; some made of fire, others of water, some of wind.

Corresponding to this are seven lands below. These range from high to low, each with its people. The land of Israel is highest; Jerusalem highest of all. The ancient lost books and the Book of Adam confirm these facts—our southern companions have read them.

Zohar 3:9b

The divine model of the earth corresponds to the heavens: everything is just as above. Rav Abba wept as he saw the fruit of a tree turn into a bird and fly off. If men knew what these things meant they would rip their clothes down to the navel—in grief, for having lost this wisdom. Even more so in relation to the rest of creation.

Wisdom is revealed through the trees, Rav Jose said. Carob, palm, pistachio, the rest—they have all been made in the same way. The fruit-bearers are all a single mystery (except for the apple), though their paths are different. The large ones that forgo fruit (except for the willows by the river) have mysteries of their own, but their sustenance comes from the same unearthly source. The small ones derive from the same mother, same heavenly sphere. And all the plants of earth, corresponding to princes in heaven, each have their own mystery modeled on heaven.

All things in this world have a mystery of their own. Since the divine one chose not to reveal it, he gave to each species a name; he made them, however mysterious, discrete.

Zohar 2:15b–16a

"DEATH WILL BE SWALLOWED UP FOREVER"

A being exists in the world that has control over a thousand keys. A female being, her heart's desire is to be near springs of flowing water, to quench her thirst.

When her time for delivery arrives, a huge snake from the upper world appears by divine will, bites into her womb, and she gives birth. The pain of labor comes from the other side, a token of the world's sins. Pain is the mystery of the snake, as he conveys suffering into the world. Why is a snake necessary? you may ask. He opens a way for souls to come into the world.

The mystery of the snake is that the woman bears souls through him. He corresponds to the body as she corresponds to the soul—as these entities come together. One day the snake of death will give birth to the bodies it embraces and they will be resurrected. This will happen before the seven years (seven millenniums) that constitute the pregnancy of snakes. In the sixth year (sixth millennium), as it gives birth to these bodies it will be consumed itself—for it is written: "Death will be swallowed up forever."

Zohar 2:219b–220a

While I slept I saw crowds and masses journeying to this place, and here a man with a rod stood and pointed. "Follow the trees," he exhorted. As they traveled they flew into the air, ascending to a place I could not see. The sound of many voices came from there, but I could not make them out.

When I woke I saw nothing; I was scared. Then I saw the man. "Did you perceive anything?" he asked me. All I had seen in the dream I told him. "That was the path taken by the departed spirits of the just,"

he said, "as they are about to enter the Garden of
Eden. What you heard was the jubilation of those
waiting in the Garden, thrilled at the entrance of the
just spirits. They who wait in Eden have already
been granted the form they will have in the world.

"The body in this world is fashioned from the
mixture of the four elements into the shape we
know, and in the same way the spirit receives form by
mixing with the four atmospheres in the Garden.
The body itself is taken as a garment for the spirit.
It is woven from the mixture of airs in the Garden,
which come together to construct this shape that
clothes the spirit. These four spiritual atmospheres
are interwoven into a unity, and through them the
spirit acquires its shape and is clothed. In the same
way, the body acquires form and matter through the
intermingling of the four elements of the world."

Zohar 2:13b

"The divine one knows that men will die," said Rav
Eliezer. "Why are souls sent into the world by his

will? Why does he need them?" he asked Rav Shimon.

"Many have asked for wisdom on this question," came the answer. "The souls descend into the world to reflect the radiance of the divine. Then, they ascend once again.

"Here is the mystery: When the soul ascends, the female's desire for the male is awakened. A cleaving follows, and the connection between upper and lower worlds is perfected through this union. The just and ascending soul arouses desire above when it rises, leading toward the time when all is united through the divine intercourse of the highest spheres."

Zohar 1:235a

Come watch closely. As the soul descends into our world, it arrives in the Garden of Eden and sees the radiance of the just spirits, standing in a great audience. It even travels to the underworld and hears the corrupt ones' cry of grief—none to console them. Its journey reveals the consequences of how one acts in the world.

As the soul enters into the world and begins to grow, a reflection of the divine is accompanying it, providing an image. The image grows with it. The life of a man is sustained by this image, careful to keep shadows from consuming it.

Zohar 3:43b

⬥

"Listen closely, my just man, my spiritual man, Rav Shimon bar Yohai. A mystery is being revealed to you from the higher academy. A human body takes form this way: breath comes from the divine spirit, soul from the tree of Life. Chariots of angels are driven by the wind of divine spirit, and their movements forge the structure of the body. Bones and bodily organs are formed to correspond to the structure of the chariot. But flesh comes from the other, impure side. Finally, the skin provided by heaven is stretched over everything, just as the heavens envelop the earth.

"Now, when heaven and earth are one, four elements are provided to sustain and enfold the body's life: fire, water, air, earth. In death, each part of the body returns to its source and evaporates. Yet breath from the divine spirit survives and the soul rises. The bones—the essence of the body—remain behind, coming from and corresponding to the chariot's form. Not so the flesh. While the flesh exists it is vulnerable to Lilith and Samael, but once the flesh has dissolved their power disappears with it."

Zohar 3:170a

Watch closely: From the first day, a divine soul is supplied to sustain each man and woman in the world—because a man has many accusers. No sooner has he entered the world than evil is waiting there to attend him. From that very moment, he is escorted like a dignitary everywhere, an evil instinct ready to become his guide.

Look closely: From the moment they are born

animals can take care of themselves, escaping from fire and other evils. Man, however, is capable of convincing himself to leap into flames—coaxed on by his evil instinct.

Zohar 1:179a

A king had an only son, much loved, as only the divine can love a soul. Because of this love, the king commanded that his son not associate with a woman of the night. Indeed, anyone who did so would be barred from the king's palace. Out of respect for his father's love, the son obeyed. However, nearby the king's house lived a whore whose face was exquisite and whose figure was ravishing.

"I need to be certain," the king said one day, "that my son's devotion remains strong. Contact the whore, engage her to seduce my son: I will see how loyal my son is."

How does the whore proceed? She comes close to the prince, lets her arms fall around him, then nibbles at his neck, beguiling him with all manner of devices.

Now, if the son were devoted to his father's authority, he would resist. He would fend her off, send her away—and this he has done. The father is pleased and summons his son to his official chambers, to be plied with gifts and honors. But who has opened this gate for the son to walk in glory? None other than the whore. Well, then, should she not receive honors also? Of course. Praise on all sides to her: It begins with her accomplishment of the king's command, and it ends with empowering the son to secure all this favor—as well as to keep the king's great devotion.

Now watch closely. Without an accuser, the just could not inherit the heavenly gifts in the world to come. All glory to those who encounter the tempter—even as much as to those who avoid temptation. All happiness to those who meet him and prevail, securing rescue. For the evil one has pointed out the gate through which they will pass; he has opened the way to unrivaled delights in the world to come.

Zohar 2:163b

THE WOMB OF
DREAMS

The way a horse does, King David drowsed, and
when he slept it was short. Now listen to how King
David avoided the taste of death in his life. Sleep
resembles death after the sixtieth breath, but
David's spiritual position required in life that he
never sleep for more than sixty breaths. In the first
fifty-nine breaths man remains in the living state,
but then he tastes the power of death and evil, and
falls under the command of an impure spirit.

So King David was vigilant and avoided the taste
of death; it would have placed him in service of the
other side. Fifty-nine breaths establish the mystery
of life in the upper world—and the sixty heavenly
breaths upon which life depends. But with the next
breath the mystery of death has begun.

As earthly stand-in, King David must avoid death

especially after midnight–the period of the She-kinah's heavenly intercourse, when she is aroused.

Zohar 1:206b–207a

No sooner has night begun than the Tree of Death commands the world—as the Tree of Life ascends to a higher sphere. During the authority of the Tree of Death on earth, all men and women taste the power of death. But humanity expects it, trusts it with their souls, as the Tree of Death holds the souls of all humanity and everyone tastes death's power. Although all these souls are in its debt, the Tree of Death rewards each sign of trust—each is restored to its holder.

When? When the Tree of Life is stirred to return, at dawn. Stirring now, and as all of humanity comes to life, the Tree of Death releases its hold. All that was entrusted to it is restored, and the tree contin-ues its journey. Why this awakening? Because the Tree of Life rules.

Zohar 3:119a

Now watch closely. As men lie in their beds, their souls withdraw and ascend. Does each one reach the divine spheres? No. Everyone does not contemplate the face of the king. Yet the soul ascends so that all that is left in the body is a beating heart, a hint of life, as the soul tries to ascend higher. It needs to pass through many levels. As it moves through the other side, it encounters and is deceived by impure spirits. If pure, the soul that was not defiled that day ascends higher, undeterred. But if impure, it is defiled among these spirits and settles among them, rising no further. There, it is given a kind of information that appears to foretell the proximate future. But often these spirits deceive, as is their nature, and tell lies. It continues this way all through the night, and when the man awakes his soul has returned, though his dreams may be false.

Zohar 1:83a

As men sleep and taste the power of death, and as the soul ascends higher, it arrives at its proper place. There, the deeds it has done that day are weighed, probed, and then written out on a tablet.

Zohar 3:121b

At nightfall, the gates of the lower world open, and the gases emanating from malice—as from the gallbladder—reach the sleeping brain. The many powers of evil instinct spread to all parts of the body. The gates of the heart are closed to its Garden of Eden: just as the light of the eye comes from the heart, the eyes are the gates that are closed, shut to the spirits of Lilith. For if they looked within, they would control the heart and the angelic lights within, that branch through the body like a tree.

Zohar 3:222a

Now watch closely. A dream must be interpreted, or else it remains an unread letter. Look closer. If unremembered, a dream is as never seen. Forget a dream and no enrichment from its interpretation will come to you.

While some dreams are true to the core, most are complicated by false things mixed with true.

Watch closely. A man who remembers a dream desires to tell it to his friends, so they will share in its interpretation. Here words and desire can join. Desire is anticipation, the beginning of everything, while words that are spoken are everything's fulfillment.

Look closely. After an impure soul is given false information of the proximate future, the man awakes and hears what the soul tells him. That is why an unjust man may see a good dream that is entirely false, luring him away from the path of truth. Drawn away, the impure spirits deceive him—as if he has wished to be deceived.

Zohar 1:199b–200a

⟨⟨✦⟩⟩

There are many kinds of dreams, many secrets, and each belongs to the secret of Wisdom. Look closely: some are dreams, some are visions, some are prophecy.

Recall that a dream uninterpreted remains an unread letter. Which does this mean: the dream will be fulfilled unknown to the dreamer, or simply unfulfilled? It will be fulfilled without being revealed—the dream has a power of its own, and the dreamer need not know it. Everything that happens in the world is contained in a dream, announced by a message. All is first declared in the heavens, extending from there into the world—expressed there in a message.

Zohar 1:183b

⟨⟨✦⟩⟩

There are angels assigned to the souls of the just at night, guiding them up into the world above. All the

souls arrive together and are pulled into the Shekinah's womb—as if she swallowed them, or was
impregnated like a woman. Then she gives new birth
to them, so the soul is as new as it was in the beginning. This event of the night is matched during the
day: new souls are created from the heavenly intercourse above.

Zohar 2:214a

FROM THE BOOKS OF BRIGHTNESS AND CREATION

[131]

Divine Glory? Here is the dream: Leah found herself in bed with a great king. "My father is on his knees with joy," she thought.

The king, impassioned for Rachel, showered Leah with attention in the dark room. Witnessing his blind love in the morning, the king confined Leah to his rooms.

His knights were in awe of the king's zealous love for Leah. When the sons to whom she gave birth could walk, they would ask the king every day, "Our mother, where does she stay?" And each day the king answered, "She can't be seen now."

So the boys' longing for Leah grew: "We bless her wherever she may be."

❦

The boys are the great poets. The king, their father, was dear to them beyond men: he taught them how to possess their mother—she, the flame of all their verses.

Now the invisible Leah awakes, longing for her father. The invisible Leah, confined, hidden, diffuses divine glory everywhere.

[132]

What is the "place" to which everything belongs? Imagine a king's daughter, coming from a faraway place, so that nobody knew where she was from. When they see how exquisite Leah is, they say, "She was surely brought from the sphere of light: her acts bring light to the world."

Then they asked where she was from. "From my father's place," she answers. "He gave me to

Jacob—as if he were my brother and my son, that is how dear to me he is. As if, in darkness, I could not tell the difference."

[198]

Can we say she was named Tamar because she was female? Then why is there both male and female in the tamar—the date palm? The fruit, male on the outside, is female inside: it is cleft like a woman.

Adam was also created male and female. Lilith tried to enter his female place and found Eve already there. But when Eve was separated, Lilith would return to him.

[199]

Why did Samael come to Eve seductively? He came for her soul, but the way to enter her was clearly in intercourse. That is why he came as the snake.

During this time, Adam dreams. That is why Lilith

comes in darkness—as he awakes, he finds his seed has been spilled.

[200]

What was Adam wearing before he discovered his nakedness? He was sheathed in a skin of lucent fingernail. When he ate the tree's fruit, this fingernail skin was removed. He could see that he was naked.

And so, too, could Lilith. She came to him in a dream, the first time he fell asleep. She came to him as if from heaven, in an illusion of pleasure— because she was thrown from heaven with Samael.

[76]

Jacob loved Rachel greatly, as if a king was showering his beautiful wife in praise. She had many children and he raised them handsomely. Yet they turned bad; they went down a wrong road. So he hated them, and their mother, too.

"Dear children," their mother cried after them, "why have you done this? Why make your father hate us?" She did not stop until they regretted it.

⸻

Now they follow their father's will. Jacob was moved to love them again, as much as before. And then he remembered his great love for Rachel.

And so, even Joseph—Joseph so far away—would return to him.

[63]

There are 32 parts to the heart—which is the word's numerical value, heart = 32. These are paths, and the world was created through them. It is as if Jacob were a king in an interior chamber, one of 32—a path leading to each one.

Now what does he do? Invite everyone through these paths to his chamber? Reveal his tapestries and treasures, his inner, concealed secrets? No, he invests Joseph with all of them—as if *he* were his only *daughter*—so that all paths are in him, in her dresses and coats.

When someone wants to approach the king he need only gaze upon her. In this way, Joseph rose among kings—and as if his only daughter, Jacob would often call him "my sister" (inwardly, in his love for her). It was as if he gave her in marriage to another king, yet she was sister to him—both he and she from one place.

And sometimes he calls her daughter, as that is what she is. And sometimes, "my mother." For Rachel is dear.

[136]

Jacob was revealed the truth because he knew the fear of his father, Isaac—not fear *of* his father but his father's *own* fear. Now what was that? *Tohu*, which gives birth to confusion.

Isaac knew the fear of truth's enemy, while his son knows the truth itself: his mother is everything to

him. And when she died—that truth was now
Rachel.

[181]

Imagine, once again, that Rachel is a king's beautiful
bride. She set aside one special day a week for the
king.

"This is my day of joy," he said, many years later,
to his precious sons. "You should also celebrate this
day: It is why you are here and why you are heir. You
will inherit all these days yourselves, your *sabbaths.*"
He continued: "For you are the reasons I will stay a
king."

[124]

Why do people fold their hands in prayer? It is the
ten fingers of the hands that represent the ten
spheres: heaven and earth were sealed with them.

Also, we hold our history in our hands, from Adam and Eve to Jacob; Rachel and Joseph to David. From Lilith to Leah, to God and his mate, the Shekinah.

[155]

The seventh sphere? Israel's seed comes from here, Jacob's. The spinal cord starts in man's brain and extends down to the sexual organ, where the seed comes from.

The seed originates from above and is gathered below.

[156]

Why will it be gathered from the "ends" of the earth? Because there all seed is blended together.

Now imagine a king's son who hides his exquisite bride in his rooms. He takes riches from his father's wealth to bring to her. She puts everything away, and one day he comes to see what has been gathered from all that was blended together as his father's treasure.

What is that treasure? From the ends of the earth the seed is brought, and it is sowed by Israel (Jacob): to be gathered by him.

[163]

God has an attribute whose name is evil, or the satan, or Samael. The form of this attribute is a hand. It has numerous messengers, all named evil. Lilith is one—the hand grasping for Adam in his sleep.

[138]

What is the ultimate truth—truth's telling of itself? A power that works through thought.

Thought yields ten articulations, and the thinker is one of them.

He created ten fingers on the hands for these ten spheres. When Boaz placed his hands on Ruth's head, as daylight lit the threshing floor, she was the one who embodied Israel's kingdom, the progenitor of David. David, the kingdom, is the thinker's dearest articulation, the final sphere.

Ruth fell to his feet, so ten blessing fingers might express Israel's need as his: to make a space for the ten spheres, their necessity in the day's embrace.

[126]

What are the spheres open to our apprehension? Three are known, and they are three legions as well, and they are three regions. The first region is light and its living reflection, water. The second is the region of spiritual beasts and the divine chariot, its great wheels.

And further in, all creatures above bless the king, fierce and frightening—he is crowned with "holy" echoing thrice.

Yet none see him—like Leah on her wedding night. In her invisible way, she will see to Joseph's birth; she, through her sister Rachel. And the third region: bedazzled Jacob.

[8, 58, 80]

The number of parts in a man's body is 248, which is the numerical value to Abraham's name. Man was completed in this name, deserving life in another world, as if another element. For there he would resemble God in structure, completed in all parts.... Insufficient, the name of evil will rot. And what truly rots, the name or the body? Yes, the body of an evil one.... God cut the covenant on his body, between his hand's ten fingers and his foot's ten toes. This shamed Abraham. But God said to him, "With my covenant in the midst of your body you will father many nations."

[3, 7]

The spheres are ten, invisible counterparts to the ten fingers—five countering five. Between the hands is the word of the covenant, centered on the tongue, inscribed on the male organ.

❦

Joseph placed himself in the middle of the ten brothers, five on each side, as they came to his house in Egypt, not knowing him. As he began to speak, tears flowed. He spoke of a wife named Rachel. Not knowing he was Joseph, the brothers were startled their mother's name was similar. "Since she has died," Joseph continued, "my body has longed for no other woman. She is mother to my memory: I keep her there but may not enter."

❦

Of the ten spheres, the last has its berth in the first, as the flame is anchored in the coal.

Part III

HOW TO RECEIVE THE KABBALAH

In the popular television series *Touched by an Angel*, three angels in human form, including the angel of death, try to show people how to live as created beings—and sometimes, how to die. As we approach the millennium, this program is joined by a number of other series that focus on the spiritual and supernatural, and the problem of leaving the body. I am thinking of *Highlander, Buffy the Vampire Slayer, Charmed*, among others, all of which try to solve the problem of leaving the body through the prism of right and wrong or comedy and romance. But no matter how much comedy there may be, these shows and their characters all take themselves very seriously. Death can never quite be looked at long enough to find a transformative place of play and irony, such as Job found in the Bible. Heresy does not exist in these shows, which, despite surface appearances of leather, long hair, or ethnic diversity, in many ways are just as conservative as the organized religion they appear to resist. There is no playing with death.

In our first stories—the stories of the Bible—it is only when human beings find that place of play and irony that they warrant the full attention of God. When Job speaks, God speaks, too. The Kabbalists knew this and transformed the texts and spiritual traditions of Judaism into a new script, which frequently baffles us at the millennium as we sit in front of our various media looking for a sign of how to live life or prepare for death. Or rather, control it. Although we pride ourselves on being "civilized" and modern, most of us go around looking for signs. We search the talk shows, the museums, the churches and synagogues, the universities, the nature trails, the malls, the crackhouses, the nightclubs, the state houses, and the bookstores for something that will resonate and lead us to either a better life, a better self, or some kind of better feeling inside. The Kabbalists took this insatiable quest for signs and betterment and turned it inside out. Yet so many of us try to read the Kabbalah as we read everything else in our lives. The Kabbalah resists, however, and causes some to seek out special teachers to unlock the mysterious signs within its texts. But is the Kabbalah really so hard to read?

Apparently so. It is not unusual to observe a standing-room-only crowd pay twenty-five dollars a person to attend a seminar on "Kabbalah and Dreams." A rabbi says to them, "When we dream, the soul leaves the body. This is a dangerous time for the soul because it is unprotected." Do they hear that dreaming is like dying? Rarely. They came to learn how to uncover the signs in their dreams. Why? To live a better life, to have more success. The rabbi hears the rustling in the seats. "My friends, we are now ready to learn more about dreams." He would like to talk further about what happens when the soul leaves the body—to read more from his texts—but someone yells out, "What does it mean to dream that my hat is burning in a fire in my basement?" The rabbi replies he will not address actual dreams because it is a very spiritual thing to interpret someone's dream. He will merely talk about dreams in general. But the crowd cannot resist. "What does it mean to dream that my wife, who lived her whole life in the Bronx, is marrying another man in a ceremony in Venice, California?" So, the rabbi relents and hands out the meanings of dreaming about hats, fires, basements, weddings, spouses, and beach towns. This is practical Kabbalah, which is only concerned with success and career, not with failure. More important, it reads its texts literally. Dreams are data that equal something. They are signs of something we want or don't want.

> When the soul leaves the body, it first transmits an account of its actions in life, and this is prepared together with the body. This event ensues from the arrival of the Judgement Day, when the book of records opens and the accusers emerge. The snake also is brought forward, prepared to bite into the body, the limbs terrified and trembling.
>
> From the *Zohar*

"What does the snake mean?" I hear a member of the audience ask. I am daydreaming now. The seminar on dreams has long since abandoned the *Zohar* to enumerate the various images of dreams. The rabbi has become a talk show host in my daydream and he is telling the audience, "When we come back, the secrets to success, hidden in the mysterious books of the Kabbalah. Our guest will show you how to conquer failure—and death—to avoid and charm the snakes of disaster." Conquer death? I realize that for practical Kabbalah, failure *is* death. The most important thing is to be a success—that is where immortality and spirit are to be found.

The commercial is over and the show is back. But it has become the Oprah Winfrey show and I'm watching "medical intuitive" Caroline Myss speak about how to discover your spirit. Suddenly, the medical intuitive's voice seems to merge with the rabbi in the seminar: "Always remember your deathday, keep heartbreak in your mind—and your body will be free of it." Another quote from the *Zohar*. A member of the audience stands up and complains of headaches. Myss tells him that the headaches are coming from his liver. She turns to the audience, "What a thing for me to say. But you see, he is suffering from disappointment. His friends continually disappoint him and he expects it to be otherwise. This is not known to him—except through his body." I marvel. Even I, without the headaches, feel transformed. This time, I am encountering creative Kabbalah.

"It is written in the *Zohar*," Myss tells the audience, "that 'when the soul has departed from the body and the body is bereft of a spirit, it is forbidden to leave the body unburied....While the body remains unburied the soul cannot come into the presence of the divine or enter a different body in a transmigration, for the soul is unable to acquire another body until the first is buried.'"

My daydream continues. Oprah turns to the audience and says, "But what does that mean for us today, Caroline?"

"It's not hard," Myss replies. "This is a text written back in the Middle Ages, but we can see how long the great teachers among us have been aware of how much the body needs a spirit and how much we need one in order to evolve and grow. This is about our personal growth and what has to be buried or dealt with in order to reach our spiritual potential. At the end of that passage I just read, it also says, 'It is like a man whose wife has died. It is not right for him to marry another before he has buried the first.' In other words, we have to face up to the disappointments in life in order to move on. They have to be buried. This is not an act but a process. We have to live our disappointments in order to live our lives. If we live them, they can be buried. If we don't, as it says in the *Zohar,* our bodies are bereft." Oprah interrupts, "In the next segment, how to know when or what to leave behind—when we come back with medical intuitive Caroline Myss."

This is what some part of me would have wished the seminar on dreams to be. Interpretive, yet personal. Some attempt is made to read the metaphors of the Kabbalists and provide a context for transformation. One might even say that the *Zohar* becomes therapeutic in the hands of the creative Kabbalist. Oprah Winfrey may provide our best translation into popular culture of the creative Kabbalist. She has enacted a serious renewal of spiritual movements, which have always been about creating an alternative to civil and traditional religion. For her, the *Zohar* would be a creative Kabbalah, offering guidance to formulating a personal religion, except Oprah would take exception to being associated with religion. Above all else, she wishes to preserve something of the creative principle, with the goal of restoring and transforming the self, and, in the process, the culture. Her great antecedents could be said to be Emerson and Whitman, who flirted with a distinctively American spirituality.

In some ways, then, Oprah offers merely another version of spiritual revival movements in this country. As she has lately added ritual to her show, she has encountered her first major criticism from those who represent traditional religion and literal interpretation. She cannot understand the literalists, yet she is one. Although she reads interpretively and creatively, there is still one thing that is literal: the self. The creative Kabbalist continues to read the self and personal spirit literally, and as I daydream my fantasy of an Oprah Winfrey Kabbalah show, I uncover my own wish to keep that domain sacred. The writers of the real Kabbalah did not let even that wish go unexamined. The real secret to the Kabbalah is that you know you can read it when you can laugh at yourself.

So what is the wish to keep the self, oneself, solemn and sacred? I must go back to my daydream and the reading of the *Zohar* on leaving the body, which Caroline Myss recited. She spoke of transmigration as personal growth and spiritual evolving. Unless you believe in reincarnation, it's easier to believe in honing your spirit or becoming a better person. That is, until you read the part about it all being "like a man whose wife has died." All the talk about discovering my spirit made me forget that this part of the *Zohar* is about the problem of leaving the body. I realize now that the creative Kabbalist in me has just as tight a grip on the wish not to leave the body as the practical Kabbalists. I think to myself, what a laugh the real authors of the Kabbalah could be having on me. They really had me going. All through the passage they speak about the hurdles in front of the soul in its effort to find another body or enter the divine presence. It seemed so problematic that I didn't realize how possible I believed it to be. The author of this text is playing with a great myth, building it up and then bursting it with "a man whose wife has died." In the end, the least he can do is put her in the ground before he takes the next one. Sublime? Hilarious? Or, as I would prefer to acknowledge, both. The full spectrum of human response.

In the *Zohar*, we have a droll but also sublime synthesis of the literal and nonliteral. Each time, we are brought back around to seeing ourselves, and the test is whether we will laugh or cry. We must learn to sustain a paradox. Where the authors seem to be talking about the soul, they are really talking about the body. What is figurative is not the body; it's the soul. The body is literal. A man has a dead wife who must be buried before he can take the next one. We must admit to holding a fantasy in ourselves: the idea that the soul is more real than the body. The only reality is that you have a body that will die and be buried, while living bodies will go on without you. But that is not all we have, however. We have the *Zohar.*

This way of reading the *Zohar* is what we may call frontier Kabbalah. It is concerned with ideals of creating a new culture or texts of wider range. Its aim is something bigger than earth or heaven. In the episode called "Leaving the Body," we seem to be confronted with a story of the soul's journey, yet we never seem to leave the body behind. The conventional divisions between the lower world of the body and the upper world of the soul are gradually broken down in a back-and-forth motion between body and soul. This motion is not found, it is created. It is a literary creation. We realize it when the story seems to become another story of "the man whose wife has died." But how is this bigger than either heaven or earth?

Well, it's like the story of the man whose wife has died. That is, we need a story to understand a bigger story. We need an author who can open up our world, make us conscious of a world bigger than our own. Why does consciousness make for a bigger author, a bigger story? To help ourselves answer this question, we can think of Shakespeare, who in so many of his plays suddenly calls the audience's attention to itself and to the fact of the play. Rather than being deflating, these moments are some of the most poignant, as we come to see ourselves and our lives as something like a play. Indeed, the bigger truth is that "the play's the thing." Why? Because to say "the play's the thing" is to sustain two states of mind at once: an utter belief in the life we are living and what we think in our minds and feel in our hearts, and, at the same time, the sense that our life and the thoughts we produce are a part of time and space, not the whole of it. Shakespeare's Hamlet duels in the end with complete seriousness and intent to win and to undo the loss of his father—even though he knows this cannot be undone and it could cost his life. And when he is poisoned, he says to Horatio, "I am dead." He is both alive and dead in his mind. His soul must leave the body. Horatio chooses not to kill himself, to stay alive to tell the story of what happened, of how Hamlet came to be dead. The bigger truth is one of origins: how we came to be and came to be dead. This is the bigger story that the Kabbalah is concerned with and that the frontier Kabbalist tries to read.

This is also a cosmic story, and frontier Kabbalah is concerned with how we invest our lives with cosmic force. In "Leaving the Body," the Kabbalah says, "No man dies before he sees the divine mother—and because of its deep yearning for her the soul departs in order to greet her." What is this about? We have already been reminded that "there is nothing more difficult for the soul than to separate from the body." So why do we leave the body, we plead to know? The Kabbalah speaks directly to the pain and suffering we feel in death by explaining that we would only leave because of a feeling equal to the suffering—a yearning to see someone we could not see otherwise: our mothers, or rather, the mother of us all. Because we feel death, the Kabbalah meets our feelings with an explanation that matches how we connect ourselves with the natural world of live and dead bodies. Because we invest the world with our feelings and thoughts, the Kabbalah responds with an explanation equal to the challenge. We are given what we want, but we are also made to see ourselves wanting it. This is what makes frontier Kabbalah poignant: the complexity of having our wishes met for what we think they are and seen at the same time for what they really are. It's like the cup of water that's brought every night to the six-year-old by the mother. She knows the child is not really thirsty, but she brings it anyway, even though she knows that it's really *her* the child is after.

Practical Kabbalah tells you that the text has an answer for any need, want, or question. Mastery is promised for every mystery. As the episode "The Nonhuman World" begins, we are confronted with an almost encyclopedic entry, as we are instructed in what is to be done when a plague visits a house. The narration is a documentary on how to think and what to do: "Come now and watch. Much can be learned from even the plague. When the divine one allows a plague of leprosy to visit a house, and it rubs off from one on to the other, the plague will not leave—not even when the spirit of defilement is gone. Not, that is, until the house is completely torn down, the stones stripped from each other and the wood pulled apart." We seem to be in the world of earthly problems, which can be solved by pulling wood apart and stripping stones from each other. But immediately we are given, "Then the place may be purified. So it is with a body, limbs, and bones." Creative Kabbalah would say, "Aha! A house visited by plague is a metaphor for the body when it dies—we are being restored to the natural order of things in order to find physical and spiritual renewal." But in taking the self and spirit so literally, the creative Kabbalist misses the literal that is cosmic. The house that is "completely torn down" is not replenished or restored. It must be demolished to purify the ground. "So it is with a body," the Kabbalah says. Each body must be demolished to make way for a new body and new life. Indeed, this is what happens when a body is put into the ground, unless mummified. We begin to sense that we are not being given an answer but another question. Rather, the Kabbalah is tapping into a more basic question. Yes, why is there no body there when I go to dig it up? What happens to the body when it dies—when I die? With such a question, we are completely in the cosmic realm of frontier Kabbalah.

Any doubt of this is dispelled as we find "the divine one" speaking in the next section: "'There are many who are ranged against you,' says the divine one to Israel, 'ready to accuse you.'" We dramatically encounter the basic method of frontier Kabbalah, which does not take any cultural forms for granted. To match the cosmic level of the story, there is the complexity of a layering of different genres—documentary and commentary, and now history, as the Exile is invoked. What is the purpose of this stretching and mixing of genres? Again, it is to enact the holding of two contrary things in mind at the same time without resolving them. Why do we suffer if we are a people that the divine one knows by name? Again, frontier Kabbalah matches the feeling behind the question. Only a cosmic voice can answer a question of abandonment. The divine one becomes involved in solving our problem of suffering. First, an acknowledgment that enemies surround us. Then, a way to stay safe: "If you are turned toward me, your strength and help, you will be shielded when outside and safe inside, in your houses. You will sleep in your beds while I stand guard around them—as well as outside."

The practical Kabbalist would stop reading at this point, having found the answer of divine protection. The creative Kabbalist would be impressed by how the Kabbalah provides a means to protect ourselves from being victims in life by remaining focused on what our goals are. They will both have to stop reading, however, because they will not be able to assimilate what the divine one says next: "Come now and watch. As evil ones approach a man's door, they look up and gaze upon Shaddai, my name engraved on the doorpost with crowns embellished over the letters. The name shatters them all. They must turn and flee, in fear of a just man's door." This turns divine protection inside out as we discover that a word can protect, and one not even spoken but written on our doorpost. This word, of course, is one of the names of God. It is both stirring and funny at the same time to think that a text can be our protection. Moreover, even one word can be a text. There are no fiery swords or angels, but only a piece of text. The word provided by the Kabbalah is from the cosmic level, though, because it must be a strong and powerful piece of text to subdue our enemies. And there we have it. Frontier Kabbalah prefers to formulate new questions rather than to answer old ones. Why do we have enemies?

Where do they come from? Each question provoked by the Kabbalah leads us further back in time.

If we can ask about our enemies, we can ask about the divine one. What makes his name so powerful? In the next episode we are told, "'He causes the grass to grow,' suggests the six hundred million angels, even though they came into being on the second day of Creation." Now we have gone as far back in time as we can go for the human species. The Kabbalah grounds everything in the Garden of Eden. The drive of frontier Kabbalah is to discover our origins, and in this episode we see an unfolding into something that can encompass body and soul. To be powerful enough to scare our enemies, the divine one must be able to cause the grass to grow. But this is not told to us by one or even three angels. A big question needs "six hundred million angels." So again we are given what we want and made to see ourselves wanting it at the same time by the mythic embellishment of precisely so many millions of angels.

Will even six hundred million angels satisfy this want? If so, the story would stop here. But a frontier Kabbalist knows six hundred million will not suffice even as a mother knows that all the cups of water in the world will not satisfy her six-year-old. So why give us the angels and the cups of water? Because we need them—the need or vulnerability in the other that they represent. We need something to bridge the gap. The separations between child and mother, body and soul, death and life, enemies and God, new grass and plagues. The Kabbalah gives us the old things we need to bridge the gaps, yet provides us with a new experience of gaps and loss at the same time, one that might be an occasion for something more than a repetition of the past. So when we read as frontier Kabbalists, we read for the new experience, a new definition of desire.

For the practical Kabbalist desire is material—not only for the objects of affluence but also those of affection and belonging. In all domains, the objective is success and consummation, whether for family, love, money, or social set. Creative Kabbalah starts from a magnanimity toward failure. The objective is to renew and reform desire for the fulfillment of spirit and community. Desire is personal and communal and fully rooted in the human. When the practical Kabbalist hears the six hundred million angels, he or she is impressed by the power of a successful force that can cause the grass to grow. The creative Kabbalist hears a mantra that can ignite a desire for fusion with a creative force of renewal. One of the rituals on *Oprah* was the recent series "Wednesdays with John Gray," the best-selling author of *Men Are from Mars, Women Are from Venus.* At the end of these episodes, Dr. Gray shows the audience how to meditate: "Oh God, my heart is open to you, come sit in my heart." He clarifies that "God" can signify any personal meaning or can be substituted with another word. In the end, the preference, though, is for God. It is a fitting ritual for what has become in many ways a revolutionary talk show in popular culture. Gray calls everyone's attention to the concept of something bigger than self. This is sophisticated because he makes everything about the self an object of analysis and interpretation. And so it is with the force that is bigger than ourselves. Never has a television talk show been so interpretive. Yet, something is still missing.

As I watched these John Gray programs with anticipation, I always felt a discomfort when it came to the meditation exercise. I thought it was the invocation of God here that got me. But I castigated myself for being so literal; after all, Dr. Gray said it could stand for any creative, spiritual force. I tried it out: "Oh Goddess, Oh Mother, Oh Freud, Oh Universe, Oh Zorro [my cat]." But it's hard to beat a one-syllable word like *God*, which has such an intimate history with our civilization. And then I realized what undermined the meditation for me. Every invocation represented a force in service to the human. Even "universe" seems to be an entity made for human beings.

You could say it was the frontier Kabbalist in me getting in the way. Or you could say it was the frontier Kabbalist arguing for a new experience, a new way to bridge the gaps in my life and in my culture. For the creative Kabbalist, human culture is terribly impoverished but can be replenished by restoring one's personal spirit and the spirit of community. Remember, the spirit and the self are always literal for the creative Kabbalist, even as she interprets and thinks symbolically about the worlds around and inside her. When the Kabbalah explains the composition of the six hundred million angels, what does the creative Kabbalist hear? "They are made of fire, and yet they are also grass. How? Like grass, they grow and are cut down every day, and then they spring up again as at first." For the creative Kabbalist, the grass is not something to know, nor is it important what the author of this story believes angels have to do with grass. What the creative Kabbalist hears is the cycle of renewal and its instruction for the human spirit. The grass and the angels are there for us, if only as a homily.

But the central author of the *Zohar* fused the grass and angels, earth and heaven, to tell a story of cosmic force, to reach for new categories of thought. Ironically, it is the angels that must be explained; it is the grass that is the primary signifier. It is hypnotic to read next of the "seven heavens above us" and the seven corresponding lands below. Of the seven heavens we are told, "Stars, planets, and messengers exist in each of them. Each contains angels assembled like chariots, awaiting their Master's service. The chariots and messengers are different in each heaven: some have six wings, some four; some with four faces, others with two, and some with just one; some made of fire, others of water, some of wind." A revelation of the seven lands follows and then the summing sentence: "The ancient lost books and the Book of Adam confirm these facts—our southern companions have read them." Again, the Kabbalah leads us back in time—to ancient books, and even further, to the Garden of Eden. The reference to "our southern companions" is almost like an interruption of a dream, much like when we find ourselves laboring in our dreams with some factuality or real-life concern. The author is speaking of those still in the land of origin as opposed to exile. It is like the man who tells his therapist that he dreamed of being in bed with Marilyn Monroe but all the while kept trying to revise sentences from the novel he was writing. The sentences are real and so is the novel, but they are in service to a story bigger than the man's individual conscious life. The Kabbalah is a form of dream-telling because it is only in a dream that cosmic events can take place without question, and exist alongside real events. It is only in our dreams that we can cross so easily boundaries of time, genre, and desire.

So "our southern companions" are there to remind us that we are in a dream. It is like being asleep and watching ourselves dream. The Kabbalah gives us the dream but makes us see ourselves dreaming it. It is a dream of ancient books, a time of different desire, a far-off experience—so ancient it is like a dream to us now. But only a few of us remember the dream, and the authors of the Kabbalah were among them. In the next passage, we continue with the dream and, this time, its dreamer: "The divine model of the earth corresponds to the heaven: everything is just as above. Rav Abba wept as he saw the fruit of a tree turn into a bird and fly off. If men knew what these things meant they would rip their clothes down to the navel—in grief, for having lost this wisdom. Even more so in relation to the rest of Creation."

Again we are returned to the Garden of Eden with a particular attention to the special knowledge we lost when we separated from it. The creative Kabbalist might be able to read this; the practical Kabbalist would never be able to, because the passage seems to value a knowledge other than that associated with success. Moreover, there seems to be an importance to thinking about a loss or failure of some kind in our history. The rabbi is weeping, and the story is told in such a way that we are made to wish that we could weep as he does. A witness has entered the cosmic dream of above and below and we are watching him weep at a loss that he alone seems to know that we have suffered. This is frontier Kabbalah, and the loss that it acts out for us cannot be repaired by "remembering the spirit" as our creative Kabbalist, Oprah Winfrey, would have it. The creative Kabbalist in me wishes it were so. There is something wonderful about feeling that we are being reminded of a unifying creative principle in such a passage. Fruits turn into birds and we are all connected. We are one with creation. But this way of reading creation is cultural and the connection is spiritual—manmade. This is not the knowledge mourned by the rabbi in the story. After all, we can easily have the wisdom of the creative Kabbalist if we just remember our own spirit and practice it. But in the story, the fruit and birds are more real than our human occupations. That is why the rabbi mourns. Again, we have the use of paradox by the author. What we expect to be symbolic is actually literal. The fruit of a tree does indeed turn into a bird and fly away. How this is so is a literal knowledge of how trees attract birds, who then eat their fruit and spread the seeds, and thus propagate new trees by virtue of their excrement.

This, too, is a form of cultural knowledge, frontier Kabbalah would say. We would need a science of ecosystems and species to tell the story of fruits turning into birds. The Kabbalah says, though, that there was an ancient time when we would have told the story as if we were a part of it. And that is what we read here:

"he saw the fruit of a tree turn into a bird and fly off." This is a way of seeing and feeling when we were still part of the Garden of Eden and had not yet traded natural for cultural knowledge. Rav Abba remembers this way of being, and it is told to us as if it were a dream we were watching.

For this kind of knowledge to be a part of us now, we must be in dreamtime. The authors of the Kabbalah knew that it was only through enacting dreamtime that they could take us back to a deeper time—the Garden of Eden and the scenes of our origins. This is called "deep time" by scientists today. But it was performed for us in writing by Kabbalists in the Middle Ages and preserved for us to read centuries later. Deep time is something different than the history of progress that the practical Kabbalist would look for; and different than the history of human intimacy, community, and reparation that the creative Kabbalist would point us toward in our personal and civil searchings. Deep time is resolutely about the nonhuman, and, one might say, the human as nonhuman. But how can this be the case for the Kabbalah when it repeatedly invokes the mystery of heaven to explain the mysteries of earth?

In an episode that follows, we read that "all the plants of earth, corresponding to princes in heaven, each have their own mystery modeled on heaven." Another holder of the dream, Rav Jose, has just told us that "Wisdom is revealed through the trees": "Carob, palm, pistachio, the rest—they have all been made the same way. The fruit-bearers are a single mystery.... The large ones that forgo fruit (except for the willows by the river) have mysteries of their own, but their sustenance comes from the same unearthly source." It is disorienting to read this passage, in which the biological and preternatural or mythic are mixed so freely. Yet we are drawn to this uniting of fact and feeling in our popular culture. We are excited by it when we watch people like the medical intuitive Caroline Myss on the Oprah Winfrey show. The creative Kabbalist has remembered the form of the dream but not its purpose. Oprah Winfrey gives her audience a cosmic mystery in the form of Caroline Myss to help unlock the mystery of the self for her viewers. The frontier Kabbalist gives us a cosmic mystery to match the feelings of mystery we have about the world.

Do we perhaps prefer the feeling of mystery to something else? There is the grief of Rav Abba and the mystery of Rav Jose. If we were to peel back the feeling of mystery, we would find a feeling of loss. Remember, it is Rav Abba who speaks of knowing the meanings of things like fruit turning into birds. A mystery is something we can keep alive, worship, or try to solve. A loss is something that would make us rip our clothes "down to the navel." Loss makes us feel like babies—helpless. So, the Kabbalah tells us that "all things in this world have a mystery of their own." But that is not all of it. Because "the divine one chose not to reveal it, he gave to each a name...." Again, we have the God that gives us names and shows his power through pieces of text. In finding the name-giving God we are jarred a little out of the dream, just enough to realize that Rav Abba must also be weeping for a time when we knew the fruits, trees, and plants without needing names. The frontier Kabbalist can be wrapped in the dream and still enjoy the irony—that what is below is above, what is low is high. The lower world is more mysterious than the upper world. The trees are the wise ones; the plants are heavenly princes.

The presence of Rav Abba and Rav Jose here ground us in one other particularity besides the trees and plants. In a way the story is all about ground. The rabbis, we are reminded, are from the ground of Europe and exile. But their eyes are on the ground of origin, and there can be no more original ground than the Garden of Eden. Every Jewish home was fraught with danger in the Middle Ages and the Renaissance. The other side of danger is mystery, and the author of this passage fills it with mystery. The author is a psychologist of exile—and a therapist of vulnerability and dread.

Everything threatened the physical and cultural life of the Kabbalists. They knew better than anyone the craving for mystery and revelation—anything to stave off the deadness. So we are shown up again by the Kabbalists. Whereas we are caught in mysteries of awe, fear, or the lottery of success, the Kabbalists use mystery to see themselves and to reimagine what is lost. This is a complex and decidedly literary turn of mind—what we would call postmodern today. Contrary to what is commonly believed in our academies, the postmodern does not have to eschew the natural or the scientific, but may play with it in order to travel the dream, to reimagine desire and restore lost worlds for further study.

It can be a wild and scary ride to travel the dream. In fact, those who have taken us for this ride have often been called wild men. Freud, for example, is considered even wilder today than in his time. Always considered a scandal for his obsession with dreams and sex, now he's also called a liar and charlatan, best buried before he corrupts society any further. King David was viewed as something of a wild man himself, hanging out with outcasts, writing poetry to God, dancing in the streets naked, acting for the dream instead of for success, risking everything for the dream of Bathsheba. And perhaps the wildest thing of all, he presumed to restore a lost world of Jewish origins through a renaissance he started with his kingdom. This was an audacious dream, because it forced other cultures to consider the Jews as an ancient culture, old and important enough to warrant a renaissance.

The Kabbalists are not quite considered wild men, at least not anymore, now that New Agers feel they have something in common with them. But it was not always that way. Today, traditional Judaism makes a space for the Kabbalah, as it tries to make spiritualism relevant again for the modern man and woman. But for most of this century the Kabbalah was repressed, as defenders of the faith and culture tried to protect us from its wildness.

What is this wildness that was so threatening? Was it overblown? Is it perhaps tamer than supposed—as we are told now by the new academics and teachers of the Kabbalah? The answer is no; it is wilder. I have tried to hold myself apart from the wildness by parceling out the Kabbalah in packages of "practical," "creative," and "frontier." This may be authentic commentary, and true to my experience of the alternative ways of reading the text. But it is also true that I was not sure I could travel the dreams that lead to the wildest dream of all in the Kabbalah. The one that gave this book its title.

It is a dream of Rebecca and Isaac and a parceling of a different kind. Isaac is telling Rebecca of a dream that "consumes me." He parcels out the dream as if it were a secret. Indeed, we are told that it is such as the story opens with what seems like a divulgence: "A child was born of Isaac's dream and nocturnal emission. Rebecca did not know it. The secret consumed Isaac; he couldn't sleep. Finally, he planned to tell Rebecca at a dinner arranged for themselves in private (he ordered a stew prepared)." I do not know if a practical Kabbalist could even read this by beginning here. There is immediately the mixing of literal and nonliteral, the mixing of real and not real, and there is the paradox that the dream, and not the nocturnal emission and its evidence, is more real, more consuming to Isaac. Moreover, as readers we are immediately drawn into the anxiety with the announcement that a "child was born." Yes, we can dream and we can have a wet dream, but are children ever born of them? This part of the story is passed to us as literal. We take it because it nags at something in us. To add to our anxiety, can we really be sure that the dinner being planned with Rebecca is not a dream, too?

A practical Kabbalist could not read this episode properly because there must be a yielding to the dream, to a lack of control that goes against everything such a reader lives for. Lives for? Yes, you opened this book because you either believed you had something to live for or wanted to find out how to get it. We all want something to live for. The practical Kabbalist wants success; the creative Kabbalist wants spirit and community. What each wants is control or a safe place to be out of control. For the practical Kabbalist, success both imparts control and makes it safe to be out of control. The creative Kabbalist finds both through revivals of spirit and community.

And what about the frontier Kabbalist, who lives for seeing in unexpected ways, opening up our possibilities of experience? Even this kind of reader wants control. The difference is that the frontier Kabbalist is aware of this desire and what and who is behind it. So what's so great about seeing yourself that naked? It is precisely this question that this story tries to formulate for us.

What Isaac tells first is of a seduction by a woman—just as he is reading the Garden of Eden story in a scroll. This woman is no doubt Lilith, the female version of the snake in Eden (among other things she represents). From this moment, the story has taken dreams and gone to the cosmic level, the other side of angels. This is the side of dread and vulnerability. The dream travels this "other side" and the way into it is the wet dream of Isaac.

This seduction goes on and on between Isaac and the woman, until he no longer needs to summon her by picking up the scroll to read. We believe it goes on and on, but we are in the dream now with Isaac and have forgotten it is only one dream. But the dream is so real we have also forgotten it is a dream. We can hear Lilith when she sidles up to Isaac like a demonic Mae West and says, "You, scrollworm…I can read your mind."

We both crave and fear someone who can read our minds. We read of Isaac's own fascination and dread with this omnipotent object. First he is trapped in a tent with her in the rain. But he cannot help it because his scroll becomes her face and arms. And then the rain ends and he is "overexposed in desert sun." He falls from what seems like a great height, though he only knows it because of "a sinking feeling inside, spirit sucked out in the cold damp air."

The story shifts as a child appears one night instead of the woman. It is a baby girl. When Rebecca and the child see each other, they both start screaming. Rebecca throws her out. We could almost laugh at this point, as we picture Isaac in the middle of this screaming and his wife throwing the child out as if she were throwing out the "other woman." But to think you could stop here would be like thinking that you could stop with the farce in a good blues song. In fact, we are told later that Rebecca and Isaac have been drinking some new wine. Rebecca may here look like a kabbalistic "whiskey-drinking woman," but there is more to the song than the melody. Beneath that screaming and throwing the child out is a wail, and we hear it when the child's scream turns to a screech outside the dwelling. With the child out of control, Rebecca takes a carver knife to the screeching. The detail belies the fantasy, as we hear along with Rebecca the story Isaac tells: "You went down, returned with her, placed her on the kitchen table and with the carver lopped off her limbs and sawed through the neck.

Yet the head still wailed, the limbs flailing. All the while I'm frozen in disbelief, in fear of you; I can't move. You gather up the pieces, force them into a pot, light the fire, boil them."

Our shock at what the dream is becoming is interrupted slightly as we are told that Rebecca adds "vegetables and spices" and orders Isaac to cut up the vegetables and set the table. As Isaac obeys and tells us that he does, we have the sensation of watching the dream, of watching ourselves dreaming. But instead of waking us up, this only makes us drop further into the dream. However, Isaac and Rebecca are awake. Isaac is looking for Rebecca's reaction, but she is "unfazed" by his dream and returns him and us to the fact of the nocturnal emission: "You reproach yourself in your dreams but I have seen the results; I cannot hide it. I find your dried seed in the sheets in the morning. If you must have wine—no more than a glass."

Nonetheless, her explanation is overshadowed as her warning expands, matching the intensity of the story, the seduction, the screaming, the emission: "But Isaac, this is dangerous. You should not think of it. Put it out of your mind." The story nags at us again as we begin to feel that there must be something real about dreams, that it is not "just a dream" after all. We are sure of it when Rebecca throws her wine glass to the floor as she realizes they are drinking the same wine that had made them drunk the night of Isaac's dream. There is a knock at the door and a blind man is there motioning for food. He is invited in but does not eat the food Rebecca offers. Is the child really cut up in the stew, we wonder? If so, is the visitor really Lilith's double, Samael—the true father of the child? Isaac screams, imploring Rebecca to get rid of the man, saying he was in the dream, too. Except Isaac was the blind man and could still hear the child's voice from the stew: "I have lost my heart and you will lose yours. To the end of days, the end of all flesh, all living hearts must be broken—a piece broken off and eaten, sticking in your throat."

Finally, Isaac gets a reaction out of Rebecca. She groans and clings to him in response and we are told "these old ones twined together as ancient vines." The author of this story has gotten a reaction out of us as well. We have awakened at the end of it as if it had been real, wishing for someone to cling to, but if we were to tell our mothers or wives, would they need someone to cling to just like us? Who can we tell it to and is there any good in the telling?

You wanted a book like this about the Kabbalah because, like me, you had a feeling you had experienced dreams of being eaten alive. But you wondered if you could fully know this experience, and if it would matter. Like me, you had the feeling that dreams are real, but you kept this a secret. You fought or held back something that felt as if it could get out and expose you—perhaps even destroy you. You were in disguise—and now you know it. So what's so great about seeing yourself? Nothing, except you know you are in disguise now and you are in the company of a few others who have seen the other side. Do I mean there really is an "other side"? Yes. This story is all about the other side. We have an absolute dread of the other side and the Kabbalah takes us seriously by giving us the elements for a story that can match our dreams and the feelings beneath them.

But what is the other side? It is whatever we dread in historical time and try to defeat. The Kabbalists were part of a culture that lived in dread of pogroms. Cultures like that might create disguises. They might give us things like the Kabbalah or African-American blues. For some of us, it is the mind that is the other side—the thing dreaded. For a while we think it is our dreams, our job, something we are afraid of on the way from point A to point B. But it is really the mind that we dread. It is like the child in Isaac's dream. It cannot be shut up no matter how we slice it or know it. Even Rebecca could not quiet Isaac's mind when she figured out it was the new wine that had provoked the wildness in the dream. The story ends with them both scared, and that is why dreams are real. Because the thing that dreamed them—the mind—is real. As is the thing that created the mind, whether we call it God, Earth, or the evolutionary ecosystem. It depends on the time of your disguise.

Although the story travels the dream to the other side, it then shows us how to work our way back to a different place. We started with our minds, but if we have been reading as the author of this story reads, we should find ourselves wanting to read more about creation instead of more about minds. We must learn to read the "ancient vines," for that is what we are, that is part of where we came from. We can try to disarm the other side with knowledge and more knowledge. But there can never be enough knowledge.

The child will always be speaking from the stew. Thus we must be more than knowledge bearers, we must become readers. And what is a reader? A reader is like Rav Abba, who "saw the fruit of a tree turn into a bird and fly off."

This kind of reading involves weeping, because there is heartbreak at the center of the dream of deep time. We can travel the dream and read the fruits that turn into birds, but we are not part of such things the way we were in the beginning. Rav Abba must speak in disguise now, and so must we if we have traveled to the wildness of the dream. This is what is in between human time and deep time. The Kabbalah is wilder than most will tell you because it is literally about wildness. It occupies the in between; it waits on the uncertainty of letting ourselves travel the dream and a new desire. It restores a lost creation to work through to a new state of creation, where desire is redefined as wanting to see fruit turn into birds and Rebecca and Isaac twine together like ancient vines. Wild is literal nature in the Kabbalah, and we who want to be enveloped from head to toe in human culture will refuse the dream and feel cheated that "dreams of being eaten alive" were just that.

Part IV

NOTES
COMMENTARY
BIBLIOGRAPHY

NOTES AND COMMENTARY

Layers

The most important thing to say about the Kabbalah is that it is always the wrong idea to clarify it. This is where the majority of books about the Kabbalah meet their downfall. Instead, the Kabbalah achieves its transparency by a momentary convergence of a multiplicity of lenses, each one of them splendidly opaque. Thus the major book of the Kabbalah, the *Zohar*, is probably the most layered text among the world's literatures.

One of the *Zohar*'s layers is the Hebrew Bible, on which it is structured as a commentary. Yet there is a greater resemblance between the imaginative powers of the authors of the Hebrew Bible and of the *Zohar* than there is between their respective beliefs. An exception is the belief in inspiration, which is synonymous with faith for both: an absolute faith in the creative imagination to overcome the inhibitions of conventional thought.

The literary method of the *Zohar* can be compared to psychoanalysis because both peel away the layers of defense against an insight by a method of indirection, one that is always on the lookout for a clue to either the interior life of the soul or the unconscious. The note on the *Zohar* that follows explains the Kabbalah's compositional strategy of indirection by creating frames on frames, commentary on commentary.

How does the Kabbalah explain itself? By creating more kabbalistic texts that add to its complexity rather than its mystery. I have created a parallel in miniature to this process in what I call episodes. In each episode I translate and bring together selections from a range of interpretive genres, narrative, imagery, and points of view. These selections suggest layers at the core of the Kabbalah. Since even the *Zohar's* complexity involves a knowledge of many literatures, it's better to begin by acquiring a sense of its core.

Inspiration

The Kabbalist believes that the Hebrew Bible contains layers of concealment the purpose of which is not to keep inspiration from the ordinary reader but rather to keep it from the grasp of conventional experts or literal-minded religious leaders and scholars, for whom inspiration is a poor authority. The inspiration concealed in the *Zohar*, for instance, imparts to the reader a resistance to careers and institutions. Avid study of careers or any social role conceals from the body the knowledge of its own desire to study the soul and to strengthen its soul's safety by keeping it consciously concealed through intellectual means. Thus the Kabbalah assumes the character of a counter-tradition to the dominant culture and its societal myths. It has become legendary for the powers of its writers who nevertheless remain unknown in English. The perception of Kabbalism persists: When taboos about life and death are lifted and the divide between religious and secular culture becomes illusory, a new art may emerge.

The engagement of dreams has served a similar purpose for modern writers, suggesting a counterintuitive level of consciousness. However, the pertinence of dreams to kabbalistic thought—and even to Socratic method—is still to be explored. In common with Kabbalists, Socrates exalted the questioning of conventional knowledge and of human nature itself.

The practical question returns: Is it necessary that one become conversant with all its layers in order to read the *Zohar?* I would answer yes, but also stress that it is the job of a kabbalistic translator to re-create the experience of reading such a work. In the same spirit, Moses de Leon was offering his reader the *Zohar* as if it were already a translated text. Here is one of many strategies that re-create the kabbalistic experience of reading (and, indeed, re-envisioning and revising) the Hebrew Bible. If the layperson can experience this process at the outset, I would not say that it is beyond his or her power to read the *Zohar.* Likewise, in the right frame of mind and humor, any reader can experience the abstract poetry of our major contemporary poet, John Ashbery, or the eternally fresh lectures on writing by Gertrude Stein. But no amount of study of Ashbery's or Stein's sources will help as much as an inspired change of mind, a new experience of the play of consciousness. An affinity for play and abstraction, along with a sympathy for the necessity of it, is required.

Disguise

Concealment suggests a known object hidden for safekeeping. Instead of an object, for Kabbalah concealment indicates a method of reading, a way of reorienting the human mind to read in a more natural or wild way, unconfined by the inhibitions of human culture. What is concealed is unknown, so that it can be come upon by surprise, as if by accident. In order to further this process, the Kabbalah may employ magical systems such as Gematria or numerology, which assign chance meanings to all words. But the "magic" is always in the service of discovery, adding another layer to the process. Dreams, and the delight in finding unexpected meanings in them unmediated by culture, provide another element of disguise.

This desire to come upon meaning in disguise is analogous to the wandering of the rabbi companions in the *Zohar.* They are not traveling to fixed destinations so much as digressing—as in a conversation. Indeed, their conversation becomes the means for accidents of arrival. Soon enough the true adventurer in these narratives is revealed to be the soul. Each night the vulnerable soul risks its fate as it leaves the body and wanders into the upper worlds. We remain in disguise as adventurous readers.

Visionary Authors

Some have said that the *Zohar* can't be a major work of art because, like psychoanalysis, it depends too heavily on the participation of the unconscious mind. Even after a century of psychoanalytic theory, the Kabbalah remains intellectually suspect for fear of the sources with which it plays, such as reincarnation and angels. An occasional exception, such as the shocking Harold Brodkey novella, "The Angel" (which once fell to me to edit as part of Brodkey's *Women and Angels*, 1985), these winged agents of the unconscious have been edited out of the narrowing Western canon. *Paradise Lost* or even Blake's epic poem *Milton* are not in intellectual circulation, and Moses de Leon is not a name commonly reckoned with.

Although several scholars in this century, beginning with Gershom Scholem, identify de Leon as the *Zohar*'s central author, his inspiration has been probed only as far as his thought and beliefs. The inspiration behind the uninhibited creative imagination that conceived and wrote most of the *Zohar* remains unexplored. Scholars may be intimidated by the subject of artistic inspiration, especially when the sources are religious or mythic. By restoring the process of its artistic creation, we come closer to experiencing the *Zohar*, and just as important, we begin to heal our loss of belief in the quality of inspiration.

The best argument I've read against suppressing authorship is in a recent essay by Rhonda Rosenberg. In "A Critique of the Critics of S, and a Reply to the Critics of J" (1997), she compares " 'the dream-problem' and 'the problem of dream-interpretation' in the scholarship of Freud's peers" to "what could be called 'the author-problem' and the intellectual failure on the part of our best-known scholars and critics to confront the original authors of the Bible and the culture they created." As she brings into focus the resemblance between dream-problem and authorship-problem, Rhonda Rosenberg suggests a lifting of the reader's inhibitions that reminds us why it is important to keep in mind as well the visionary author of the *Zohar*:

> *Like Freud, I confess that I have been forced to recognize that popular and ancestral opinion offers more insight into "the truth of the matter" [of the Hebrew Bible] than disquisitions of many of our scholarly experts. How can I possibly say such a thing, particularly after all the centuries of effort to break through superstitious tradition on the subject of divine authorship and inspiration? Why would I prefer notions of an old man in the sky and the "Five Books of Moses" to images of a scribal school or a great redactor tradition that compiled and recomposed the text? Because in such notions we can see, so clearly and bitterly sweet,*

a wish displaced, a problem attempted but failing to be solved. And in a way, the closer we are to seeing this, the closer we are to the original authors.

Let me try to explain. Great writers play with the wishes and problems of the human psyche and those of the culture of which they are a part. There is nothing extraordinary in such an observation but it is one often overlooked and, I would say, deliberately obscured by many contemporary scholars of the Bible. Why is it so hard for us to take in a great author? Postmodern criticism is often characterized as a killing off of the singularity of authorship. The work of the postmodern critic Jacques Derrida is usually held up in accusation and disdain on this point, but I find it interesting that the disclaimers are almost always the disposers of authorship. Derrida himself is hardly a disposer, choosing to linger in the singularity of an author. It is ironic that I became a reader of Derrida on account of those unable to read an author, particularly a biblical one. And though I am unsure yet how close Derrida comes to understanding the author-problem, what matters is that he grapples with it, and it is that grappling that is woefully missing in the scrutinies of most of our contemporary experts on the Bible.

For many centuries Moses was considered the hero of the Pentateuch, God's scribe, the author of the Bible's first five books. We have gone from myth to theory, from what Freud called notions of "the great man" to the neutered images of great redactors and objectifications called composite texts. Gone are a people's love objects, the idealized personalities of a Moses with a staff or a Yahweh taking an evening walk in the Garden of Eden. And in our detachment from these objects, we have lost sight of

175

the basic problems that the efforts of culture attempt to solve. And we have lost touch with the human, sexualized basis of culture, particularly those fully sexual individuals that give us a vital culture and keep it alive through artistic commentary and restoration.

A New History of Earth

I have interpreted many of the terms of kabbalistic myth in the context of Parts I and III of this book. To define these terms on their own can be misleading, since they are part of a way of seeing the world that has lost the primacy of its cultural setting. Imagine walking in an Ecuadoran rain forest, on the one hand, and reading a glossary of species found there in Latin and Spanish, on the other. I would italicize *Spanish* (except for native Spanish speakers) because the point of the analogy is that there is *no* native speaker of the language of the Kabbalah. Moreover, there is no equivalent of a literary Latin to be apprehended, or a Greek Neoplatonic idiom. The language of the Kabbalah is a poetic invention anchored in various idioms of ancient and medieval languages which we can only awkwardly reconstruct.

I have left the reader imaginatively standing in the rain forest for this purpose: I doubt you will want to peruse a bibliography of its species, either before or after you've entered the rain forest.

Instead, if your memory needs prompting, you may want to walk in a tropical botanic garden or view a documentary film or read a personal account of a similar visit by a scientist. That is what I've intended to provide, a personal journey of reading and translation into the wild realm of the Kabbalah as it is written.

Imagine further, a century or two from now, when human colonies exist on other planets and moons, that Earth becomes so precious as our birthplace that it is made sacred and a new religion is born. The center of this new religion is restoration, just as it had been in Judaism. The entire history of Earth will be told in the form of restoring the range of natural ecosystems, from oldest to the most recent ones following the last Ice Age. This doesn't mean the stories will focus upon extinct species such as dinosaurs, but rather that the ecosystems will be represented in some creative way that includes memory of all that has been lost. What is needed for a new religion, then, is a new history of Earth.

Now travel back merely three millennia to the time of David and Solomon. The new temple to Yahweh is one of many temples, and Jerusalem is far from being a sacred place. (We learn from the Bible that even three centuries after Solomon's death, dozens of the temples he built to the religions of his many wives are still in service.) There is no sacred text called the Hebrew Bible. At Solomon's court, many poets, historians, translators, and scholars are at work restoring the myths and legends of the Jews, translating and recomposing them in a new written language. This is happening long before the new language is held sacred by some. Restoration of the archaic cultural history is the main focus, transformed into new myths of origins in the venerable cultures of the day, Egypt and Mesopotamia.

The integrity of the stories of Adam and Eve or Abraham and Sarah did not depend on their accuracy. Rather, these stories had to be represented in a creative way that enfolded them as well as the Jewish culture into a complete history of Earth. In our time we see the beginnings of a new religion in the new languages of DNA and genomes, of ecosystems and exoplanets. How and when will the creative culture come into existence to translate these languages into a human poetics? That question was prefigured by the example of the *Zohar* in the thirteenth century.

Return to Europe and the Near East in that time, after the last millennium. A new religion is about to be born in the form of a renewal of the prophetic or visionary core of Judaism, and the *Zohar* is its Bible-in-formation. The *Zohar* is built upon the messianic dream of the legendary rabbi Shimon bar Yohai. Instead of a restoration of the Temple, what is restored is the mythic core that retells the story of heaven and earth. Our predators—the evil that came before us—are restored as well, taking the form of the dark side, the other side, the unconscious life. In the same way, a future religion of the ecosystem will explain our dreams and nightmares by illustrating the species who predate us and those who ate us, from leopard and lion to the microbes of disease. No doubt the half-beast half-man monstrosities imagined at the gates of Eden were dream images reflecting the imprint of the predators of humans who were already extinct at the time the Hebrew Bible was being written.

Scholars of the Secret

Voodoo popped up in early sound films and became a catchword, and in similar ways the word *Kabbalah* has become a catch-all to signify secret spiritual meanings. Unlike voodoo, as far as I know, the tradition of the Kabbalah produced some major works of poetry and fictional narrative in the Middle Ages that are still largely unknown and untranslated. The few translations of kabbalistic texts that exist in English give merely the bones and not the flesh of the Kabbalah. It would be like having a historian translate *The Odyssey* as if it were an arcane history text.

"The book of *Zohar,* the most important literary work of the Kabbalah, lies before us in some measure inaccessible and silent." These words, written over fifty years ago by the leading scholar of the Kabbalah, Gershom Scholem, formulate the problem for any translator and interpreter.

Scholem revealed the psychology of the Kabbalists while focusing his own creative contribution on the historical implications. Moshe Idel and Yehuda Liebes, Scholem's most significant reinterpreters, have thrown the emphasis back on the poetry of the texts and the individual reader and practitioner. Poetry may not help a community to material or political success, but the lives of its audience are enriched nonetheless. The time has come, perhaps, to translate the complex language of the Kabbalah into a psychologically vivid form.

The Torah

The Hebrew Bible divides in three: Torah, Prophets, Writings. The Christian designation of "Old Testament" contains virtually the same text as the Hebrew Bible. A significant portion of the Torah was written in the Solomonic era, at the courts of David, Solomon, and Rehoboam. Other parts of the Hebrew Bible, especially those of high literary merit (such as a version of the Book of Ruth and Song of Solomon, early Psalms, a portion of the Books of Samuel), were probably written in this era of the Solomonic renaissance (see my *The Book of David*, 1997, for elucidation of the earlier period upon which this renaissance, or cultural revival, is based).

The Torah itself is multilayered, with some of the later additions serving as commentary and reinterpretation of the older, literary portion. The books of the Prophets reinterpret the Torah as well as earlier historical books, and thus the mode of *aggadah*, or telling as retelling, had precursors long before its prominence in the Talmud and the Midrash.

Perhaps more significantly, the literary authors of the Torah, including J and other court writers in Solomonic Jerusalem around the ninth and tenth centuries B.C., sometimes wrote as if they were living in an earlier millennium. The central author of the *Zohar* also wrote as if his book were already ancient.

The Midrash

Hundreds of books over many centuries make up the Midrash. Selections from many of these books are anthologized in compilations, such as the Midrash Rabbah, which includes separate volumes devoted to each book of the Hebrew Bible. In general, the Midrash takes significant form in the centuries after the Talmud and before the *Zohar* (from the second to tenth centuries). It moves from playful exegesis of the Bible to narrative that incorporates expansive imaginative freedom as well as startling portions of ancient material that may have been either rediscovered or reinvented.

At the point that the Midrash approaches a visionary hermeneutic, it begins to react and become more conservative, inhibited by lack of a full re-vision of its sources in the Hebrew

Bible and Hebraic culture. In this way, it resembles the trajectory of modern Jewish culture, whose highlights after Freud and Scholem are either increasingly isolated fragments or conventional guides dragged out to absurd lengths—rather than cornerstones of a new vision.

The new vision begins in the Kabbalah, which is often dressed in the exegetical mode of the Midrash but in fact demonstrates a huge break with it, for the Kabbalah has new and visionary myths of its own. The imaginative payback for this break is a corresponding breakdown of conventional taboos on thought, imagery, and composition. In short, an explosion of religious and literary sensibility.

The Kabbalah

The best source for definitions of terms found in the Kabbalah is the English-language *The Encyclopedia Judaica* (Jerusalem: Keter, 1973). The entries on the Kabbalah were written by Gershom Scholem.

At the time of the blossoming of the Kabbalah in the twelfth century, the renowned philosopher Maimonides was explicating in great detail the meaning of prophecy and in particular the end of the period of biblical prophecy. The Midrash had largely filled the space of prophecy that had been previously filled by the Talmud, the Apocrypha, Hellenistic books, and others. Yet there was another genre that spanned the period from the Hebrew Bible to the Kabbalah, and that is the *targums,* or translations of the Hebrew Bible into other languages, in particular Aramaic. Most of these targums are now lost. Among those that have been saved by becoming canonical, it is clear that some of their translators were visionary poets themselves; their translations more accurately should be called transformations of the Bible into new ways of seeing. In effect, the targums kept the tradition of prophecy alive by suggesting new visions of the future.

I believe it best to attempt a visionary or experiential kind of modern translation. A reader wants to experience the world *through* the vision or myth, and not to examine and stare at the mythic system itself like some dead skeleton. Therefore, concepts and systems of knowledge that are central to kabbalistic myth—Tzimtzum, the Shells of the Nut, the Domain of the Husks, Chashmal, the Breaking of the Vessels, Ein Sof, Gnosis, Gematria, the Transmigration of Souls, among others—are often poorly explained and understood. It is futile to study definitions without wider contextual knowledge. For those who wish to immerse themselves in systems of myth, history, and philosophy, the bibliography I have prepared will serve.

The *Zohar*

Just as the great writers of the Bible were rewriting earlier myth and history, the main author of the *Zohar*, Moses de Leon, had his earlier sources. De Leon was the kind of author whose greatness rivaled the Bible's J writer, and thus he might be called a Neo-Solomonic writer of the Judaic renaissance in southern Europe. By setting the *Zohar* in an earlier millennium and suggesting authorship to a spiritually Mosaic-like figure, Rav Shimon bar Yohai, De Leon paralleled the ancient Hebraic writers.

Several layers added to Moses de Leon's *Zohar*—Zohar Hadash, Midrash ha-Neelam, and Tikkunei Zohar among them—seem to be partially written by others. Yet they might also have been written by de Leon in one of his many voices.

Propelling the mythic drama of the *Zohar* is a journey toward a realignment of heaven and earth—prefigured in each soul's cosmic journey. All the complexities of origin and destination, of thought and action, of conscious and unconscious mind, serve this larger purpose. Rather than an end of days, the future holds a new Garden of Eden, one that cannot be compared to the original for we—or our souls—have not yet encountered it. But that is not all; that is another beginning, another form of consciousness, and for that reason all the taboo bending and genre bending, the artistic forms of play and subversion found in the *Zohar*, are justifiable preparation.

The preparation must lead to a revelation, since the new Garden of Eden has always been concealed in the original Garden of Eden. Although our souls may have been back to the original Garden, they are not equipped to search for what is concealed. The *Zohar* creates framework for framework, episode for episode, teaching that we can only meet what we search out indirectly—and that our guide must also at the core be concealed, abstract, in order that a revelation be possible. Genres and institutions that are meaning-making must be used and discarded, moved aside so that we can make our way. We continue on faith, as if we are blind.

The issue of prophecy raises all the others I have mentioned. Prophecy is turned toward the future because it expects an end to time. The *Zohar* is so certain of it that tradition demands its reader be initiated as a collaborator, having acquired extensive years of study in myths and texts. At this point, accepting the future's judgment, the collaborative reader, like the author, can shed all taboo and enter the book sexually naked. For the book has become a poem outside of time—mythic—in which all borders, all genres can be blurred and remade.

Without a contemporary vision of the future, I can still insist on its necessity. Yet there is such a vision coming-to-be in frontier ecology, a way of seeing through our culture that parallels seeing through a poem—to a natural world outside. Frontier ecology allows us to see ourselves as the work of the creative ecosystem in which all life is on a perpetual journey to evolve, to go beyond itself. Because an ecosystem created a space for us, opening a niche for *Homo sapiens,* we ourselves are its poetic artifacts.

Significant writers of the Kabbalah who followed Moses de Leon further complicated or oversimplified its vision of the future, as the case may be. These authors, who lived between the thirteenth and seventeenth centuries, include Abraham Abulafia, Joseph Gikatilla, Moses Cordovero, Isaac Luria, Chaim Vital, Elijah de Vidas, and Isaiah Horowitz.

The Sefirot

I include some information on the main kabbalistic myth of the *sefirot* in order to elucidate my method of translation. I've drawn my own chart in order to show how the biblical characters I appropriate in my translation are associated with the *sefirot,* also called a "tree of life" (and to be distinguished from the Tree of Life in the Garden of Eden). The sefirotic system is also represented as *Adam Kadmon,* the unfallen or upper, heavenly Adam, and the *sefirot* are attributed to parts of his body. The usual manner of drawing a relational chart of the *sefirot* is also more suggestive of a body or a tree. However, this particular representation of the sefirotic system is in danger of becoming a visual cliché, and it too often reduces kabbalistic myth to a cliché as well.

The symbolism of the *sefirot* can be extremely complex, having gone through many reinterpretations. Kabbalists also elucidated different groupings for them. One, for instance, involves the powerful symbolism of the Seven Days of Creation. Few Kabbalists agreed with each other about the exact symbolism, and it might seem silly to a Kabbalist to draw charts for the purpose of clarification. Rather, a chart of the sefirotic system was more likely viewed as an intellectual talisman.

KETER		
Leah/Invisible	Ancient of Days (Holy One)	
	Nothingness	

BINA		CHOCHMAH
Eve	Adam... (Serpent/Samael)	
Mother		Father

CHESED		GEVURAH
Rebecca		Isaac
Abraham	Sarah... (Lilith)	
left arm		right arm

TIFERET		
Jacob	son	tree of Life
	trunk	bridegroom

HOD		NETZACH
Ruth (Aaron)		(Moses) Boaz
left leg		right leg

YESOD		
Joseph	son	seed
	phallus	bridegroom

SHECHINAH			
Rachel	daughter	David	bride
	Leah/visible		

Dreams of Being Eaten Alive

In this episode, the selections from the *Zohar* are largely about the *sefirot*—the myth of the ten emanations that encompass the distance between humans, who stand in the lower world, and the Godhead in the upper world. Each *sefirah*, or sphere of emanation, is characterized in many ways, as I have described in the note pertaining to *sefirot*. Many of these ways are systems in themselves, and I have appropriated one as a layer of narrative to help animate the more conceptual layers of commentary on the story of Adam and Eve in Genesis. The system of characterizing the *sefirot* I have emphasized is one in which each particular *sefirah* is given the identity of a biblical character. Thus, in this episode I have opened up the characters of Isaac and Rebecca. As the text alludes to the *sefirot* they represent, I have elaborated the scene of dream interpretation by folding the dreams into a further narrative layer.

The biblical character associated with each *sefirah* is given in the note on the *sefirot,* and the basic correlation of biblical characters to *sefirot* in this episode is given in this table:

Characters	Sefirot
Isaac + Adam	Chochmah + Gevurah
Rebbeca + Eve	Binah + Chesed
Jacob	Tiferet
Samael + Lilith	Chochmah

Instead of asking the reader to study the correlations, and in place of defining or creating yet newer systems of explication, I have attempted to re-create the experience of reading kabbalistically. The sense of this episode, then, resembles the texture encountered by an adept familiar with the mythical systems of Kabbalah.

Leaving the Body

The concluding selection of this episode comes from the Midrash and reveals the breathtaking dimensions of drama in the Zoharic myth of the soul by contrast with the awesome movement of interpretive scenes (at Mount Sinai, in the Temple a millennium later, and the scene of reading in yet another millennium) in the earlier biblical myth of relations between heaven and earth.

The Angel of Death Dancing

This episode layers scenes in the closing days of the life of the protagonist and attributed author of the *Zohar*, Shimon bar Yohai. The selections come from all three volumes of the *Zohar*, once again to be capped in the end by a selection from the Midrash on Genesis. Here, God, man, and Adam converse as have Rav Shimon and his companions in the *Zohar*, though more tersely. So pithily, in fact, that the realms of the upper world and of time since the creation already seem the ground in which the peregrinations of the *Zohar* are rooted.

The Power of Lilith to Consume a Child and The Nonhuman World

The world of the *sitra achra*, or other side, is represented by Lilith. The emotional gravity of her realm is given its imaginative exclamation point by the angels. In the midst of it, I have included a selection from the Midrash that suggests the way to read these realms beyond the human is to acknowledge them all as real—as arguably real as is the human imagination. Nebuchadnezzar's dragon is as real as the Garden of Eden, and both are as real as the disease of leprosy or the natural science of tree species. Did Daniel attempt to demythologize the dragon? Instead, he demolished it by the intensity of his imaginative attention: we can feel the nails in the dragon's bowels, whether or not we can verify its existence.

"Death Will Be Swallowed Up Forever"

The many layers of the *Zohar* account for the existence of the universe of endless life by focusing on the soul within the body. The soul is rendered real by analogy with the seemingly ageless world of our mind, including both conscious and unconscious realms. In the same manner, evil is rendered as necessary by analogy with the desire to explore temptation—rather than to avoid it. This desire—and the boundless variations of temptation—is to be explored imaginatively. The keys to that lifelong journey are in the *Zohar*, in the form of mysteries that seduce our mind. Beyond mere explanation, then, the mystery of death can also be solved by the analogous bodily experience of the wish to devour, or to be devoured.

The Womb of Dreams

In this episode, selections show the reader how to read; first by explaining the process of reading dreams, and then by demonstrating the process of reading our emotional or interior lives and their kabbalistic analogy, the soul. This process of reading is ultimately analogous to sexual intercourse and, further, to the cycle of birth and death. However, since the heavenly intercourse creates the soul, death is no longer of significance—just as in dreams, which end only in our waking, or rebirth into life.

The Books of Brightness and Creation

Sefer Yetzirah, or *The Book of Creation*, and *Sefer ha-Bahir*, or *The Book of Brightness*, are the oldest books we have that elaborate the mythic system of the Kabbalah, the *sefirot*. Like a book of midrash, *The Book of Brightness* is an anthology of several genres: commentary (on the Bible as well as on the earlier *Sefer Yetzirah*); parables and proverbs; dialogues; and expositions of letters of the alphabet and sacred names. Yet it is an incomplete anthology, with much missing and presumed lost, and even the thirteenth-century Kabbalists, including Moses de Leon, assumed it was a collection of vestiges that had survived from lost scrolls.

While *The Book of Brightness* in its present form can be located in the tenth century, the *Sefer Yetzirah*, or *The Book of Creation*, can go back as far as the third century, almost justifying its later attribution to Rabbi Akiva, although the latter almost certainly did not compose it.

I have selected excerpts that show the advance beyond the Midrash, in that biblical commentary is transformed into another mythical realm, often mysterious, but more often engaging the kabbalistic myth of *sefirot*. In 124 and 138, they are the "ten fingers" and "ten spheres." The focus on the body, and especially on sexual reproduction, as in 155, is also redolent of the Kabbalah, as is the realm of dreams rooted in the Garden of Eden.

BIBLIOGRAPHY

Abelson, J. *Jewish Mysticism* (New York: Hermon Press, 1969).

Abram, David. *The Spell of the Sensuous: Perception and Language in a More-Than-Human World* (New York: Pantheon, 1996).

Afterman, Allen. *Kabbalah and Consciousness* (Riverdale, NY: Sheep Meadow Press, 1992).

Ariel, David. *The Mystic Quest: An Introduction to Jewish Mysticism* (New York: Schocken Books, 1992).

Bakan, David. *Sigmund Freud and the Jewish Mystical Tradition* (New York: Schocken Books, 1958).

Bension, Ariel. *The Zohar in Moslem and Christian Spain* (New York: Hermon Press, 1974).

Berg, Philip S. *Kabbalah for the Layman* (New York: Research Centre of Kabbalah, 1981).

Biale, David. *Eros and the Jews* (New York: Basic Books, 1992).

———. *Gershom Scholem: Kabbalah and Counter-History* (Cambridge: Harvard University Press, 1979).

Bloom, Harold. *Kabbalah and Criticism* (Seabury Press: New York, 1975).

Bloom, Harold, ed. *Gershom Scholem* (New York: Chelsea House Publishers, 1987).

Blumenthal, David R. *Understanding Jewish Mysticism* (New York: Ktav, 1978).

Borges, Jorge Luis. *Selected Nonfictions;* ed. Eliot Weinberger; trans. Esther Allen, Suzanne Jill Levine, and Eliot Weinberger (New York: Viking, 1999).

Buber, Martin. *Hasidism* (New York: Philosophical Library, 1948).

Cooper, David A. *God Is a Verb: Kabbalah and the Practice of Mystical Judaism* (New York: Riverhead Books, 1997).

Cordovero, Moses ben Jacob. *The Palm Tree of Deborah,* trans. Louis Jacobs (New York: Hermon Press, 1974).

Coudert, Allison. *Leibniz and the Kabbalah* (Boston: Kluwer Academic, 1995).

Culianu, Ioan P. *The Tree of Gnosis,* trans. Hillary Wiener and Ioan P. Culianu (San Francisco: HarperSan Francisco, 1992).

Dan, Joseph. *Gershom Scholem and the Mystical Dimension of Jewish History* (New York: NYU Press, 1987).

Dan, Joseph, ed. *The Early Kabbalah,* trans. Ronald C. Kiener (Mahwah, NJ: Paulist Press, 1986).

De Leon, Moses. *The Book of the Pomegranate,* trans. Elliot R. Wolfson (Atlanta: Scholars Press, 1988).

Derrida, Jacques. *Glas,* trans. John P. Leavey Jr., and Richard Rand (Lincoln: University of Nebraska Press, 1986).

Deutsch, Nathaniel. *The Gnostic Imagination: Gnosticism, Mandaeism and Merkabah Mysticism* (New York: E. J. Brill, 1995).

Eilberg-Schwartz, Howard. *God's Phallus and Other Problems for Men and Monotheism* (Boston: Beacon Press, 1994).

Eisenberg, Evan. *The Ecology of Eden* (New York: Alfred A. Knopf, 1998).

Eleazar ben Judah of Worms. *Three Tracts,* trans. J. Hirschman and A. Altmann (Berkeley: Tree Books, 1975).

Epstein, Perle. *Kabbalah: The Way of the Jewish Mystic* (New York: Doubleday, 1978).

Fine, Lawrence, ed. *Essential Papers on Kabbalah* (New York: NYU Press, 1995).

Finkel, Bruria, and Jack Hirschman. *The Path of the Names: Writings by Abraham ben Samuel Abulafia* (Berkeley: Tree Books, 1973).

Fisdel, Steven A. *The Practice of Kabbalah* (Northvale, NJ: Jason Aronson, 1996).

Fishbane, Michael A. *The Kiss of God: Spiritual and Mystical Death in Judaism* (Seattle: University of Washington Press, 1994).

Freud, Sigmund. *The Interpretation of Dreams,* trans. James Strachey (New York: Avon Books, 1965).

Ginsburg, Elliot Kiba. *The Sabbath in the Classical Kabbalah* (Albany: SUNY Press, 1989).

Ginzberg, Louis. *The Legends of the Jews,* 7 vols. (Philadelphia: Jewish Publication Society of America, 1909).

Goodenough, Erwin R. *Jewish Symbols in the Greco-Roman Period,* 13 vols. (New York: Pantheon Books, 1953–1968).

Gottlieb, Freema. *The Lamp of God* (Northvale, NJ: Jason Aronson, 1989).

Govrin, Michal. *The Name*, trans. Barbara Harshav (New York: Riverhead Books, 1998).

Graetz, Heinrich. *History of the Jews*, 6 vols., trans. Bella Löwy (Philadelphia: Jewish Publication Society of America, 1891).

Green, Arthur. *Keter: The Crown of God in Early Jewish Mysticism* (Princeton: Princeton University Press, 1997).

Grozinger, Karl-Erich, and Joseph Dan. *Mysticism, Magic, and Kabbalah in Ashkenazi Judaism* (New York: Walter de Gruyter, 1995).

Halamish, Mosheh. *An Introduction to the Kabbalah*, trans. Ruth Bar-Ilan and Ora Wiskind-Elper (Albany: SUNY Press, 1998).

Halevi, Z'ev ben Shimon. *Adam and the Kabbalistic Tree* (York Beach, ME: Samuel Weiser, 1990).

Handelman, Susan A. *Fragments of Redemption: Jewish Thought and Literary Theory in Benjamin, Scholem, and Levinas* (Bloomington: Indiana University Press, 1991).

Hartman, Geoffrey H., and Sanford Budick, ed. *Midrash and Literature* (New Haven: Yale University Press, 1986).

Heschel, Abraham Joshua. *The Sabbath: Its Meaning for Modern Man* (New York: Farrar, Straus and Giroux, 1951).

Hoffman, Edward, ed. *Opening the Inner Gates: New Paths in Kabbalah and Psychology* (Boston: Shambhala, 1995).

Idel, Moshe. *Messianic Mystics* (New Haven: Yale University Press, 1998).

———. *Golem: Jewish Magical and Mystical Traditions on the Artificial Anthropoid* (Albany: SUNY Press, 1990).

————. *Kabbalah: New Perspectives* (New Haven: Yale University Press, 1988).

————. *The Mystical Experience in Abraham Abulafia,* trans. Jonathan Chipman (Albany: SUNY Press, 1988).

————. *Studies in Ecstatic Kabbalah* (Albany: SUNY Press, 1988).

Jabés, Edmond. *The Book of Questions,* trans. Rosmarie Waldrop (Middletown, CT: Wesleyan University Press, 1991).

Jacobs, Louis. *Jewish Mystical Testimonies* (New York: Schocken Books, 1977).

Janowitz, Naomi. *The Poetics of Ascent: Theories of Language in a Rabbinic Ascent Text* (Albany: SUNY Press, 1989).

Kaplan, Aryeh. *The Bahir* (Northvale, NJ: Jason Aronson, 1995).

Kushner, Lawrence. *The Book of Letters* (New York: Harper & Row, 1975).

Labowitz, Shoni. *God, Sex, and Women of the Bible* (New York: Simon & Schuster, 1998).

Levinas, Emmanuel. *Nine Talmudic Readings,* trans. Annette Aronowicz (Bloomington: Indiana University Press, 1990).

Liebes, Yehuda. *Studies in Jewish Myth and Jewish Messianism,* trans. Batya Stein (Albany: SUNY Press, 1993).

————. *Studies in the Zohar,* trans. Arnold Schwartz, Stephanie Nakache, and Penina Peli (Albany: SUNY Press, 1993).

Margulis, Lynn. *Symbiotic Planet* (New York: Basic Books, 1998).

Matt, Daniel C. *The Essential Kabbalah: The Heart of Jewish Mysticism* (San Francisco: HarperSanFrancisco, 1995).

————. *Zohar: The Book of Enlightenment* (New York: Paulist Press, 1983).

Meltzer, David. *The Secret Garden: An Anthology in the Kabbalah* (New York: Seabury Press, 1976).

Ostow, Mortimer. *Ultimate Intimacy: The Psychodynamics of Jewish Mysticism* (Madison, CT: International Universities Press, 1995).

Patai, Raphael. *The Jewish Alchemists* (Princeton: Princeton University Press, 1994).

————. *The Hebrew Goddess* (Detroit: Wayne State University, 1990).

Reuchlin, Johann. *On the Art of the Kabbalah,* trans. Martin and Sarah Goodman (Lincoln: University of Nebraska Press, 1993).

Robinson, Ira. *Moses Cordovero's Introduction to Kabbalah: An Annotated Translation of His* Or Ne'Erav (New York: Yeshiva University Press, 1994).

Rojtman, Betty. *Black Fire on White Fire: An Essay on Jewish Hermeneutics from Midrash to Kabbalah* (Berkeley: University of California Press, 1998).

Rosenberg, David. *The Book of David* (New York: Harmony Books, 1997).

————. *The Lost Book of Paradise: Adam and Eve in the Garden of Eden* (New York: Hyperion, 1993).

————. *A Poet's Bible: Rediscovering the Voices of the Original Text* (New York: Hyperion, 1991).

Rosenberg, David, and Harold Bloom. *The Book of J* (New York: Grove Weidenfeld, 1990).

Rosenberg, Rhonda. "A Critique of the Critics of S, and a Reply to the Critics of J," in David Rosenberg, *The Book of David* (New York: Harmony Books, 1997).

Rosenberg, Roy A. *The Anatomy of God: The Book of Concealment, the Great Holy Assembly and the Lesser Holy Assembly of the Zohar, with the Assembly of the Tabernacle* (New York: Ktav, 1973).

Rotenberg, Mordechai. *The Yetzer: A Kabbalistic Perspective on Eroticism and Human Sexuality* (Northvale, NJ: Jason Aronson, 1997).

Rothenberg, Jerome, Harris Lenowitz, and Charles Doria, eds. *A Big Jewish Book: Poems and Other Visions of the Jews from Tribal Times to Present* (Garden City, NY: Anchor Press/Doubleday, 1978).

Rothenberg, Jerome. *Poland: 1931* (New York: New Directions, 1974).

Ruderman, David B. *Kabbalah, Magic, and Science: The Cultural Universe of a Sixteenth-Century Jewish Physician* (Cambridge: Harvard University Press, 1988).

Safran, Alexandre. *The Kabbalah*, trans. Margaret A. Pater (Jerusalem: Feldheim, 1975).

Schaya, Leo. *The Universal Meaning of the Kabbalah*, trans. Nancy Pearson (London: Allen and Unwin, 1971).

Scholem, Gershom. *On the Possibility of Jewish Mysticism in Our Time and Other Essays*, ed. Avraham Shapira, trans. Jonathan Chipman (Philadelphia: Jewish Publication Society, 1997).

———. *On the Mystical Shape of the Godhead* (New York: Schocken Books, 1991).

———. *Origins of the Kabbalah*, trans. Allan Arkush, ed. R.J.Z. Werblowsky (Philadelphia: Jewish Publication Society, 1987).

———. *Jewish Gnosticism, Merkavah Mysticism, and Talmudic Tradition* (New York: Jewish Theological Seminary of America, 1970).

————. *The Messianic Idea in Judaism* (New York: Schocken Books, 1969).

————. *Major Trends in Jewish Mysticism* (New York: Schocken Books, 1967).

————. *On the Kabbalah and Its Symbolism*, trans. Ralph Manheim (New York: Schocken Books, 1965).

Scholem, Gershom, ed. *Zohar: The Book of Splendor* (New York: Schocken Books, 1949).

Silk, Dennis. *Retrievements: A Jerusalem Anthology* (Jerusalem: Keter Publishing House, 1977).

Singer, Isaac Bashevis. *Satan in Goray* (New York: Noonday Press, 1955).

Spector, Sheila A. *Jewish Mysticism: An Annotated Bibliography on the Kabbalah in English* (New York: Garland, 1984).

Sperling, Harry, and Maurice Simon, trans. *Zohar*, 5 vols. (London: Soncino Press, 1931–1934).

Steinsaltz, Adin. *The Long Shorter Way: Discourses on Chasidic Thought*, ed. and trans. Yehuda Hanegbi (Northvale, NJ: Jason Aronson, 1988).

————. *The Thirteen-Petalled Rose*, trans. Yehuda Hanegbi (New York: Basic Books, 1980).

Tarn, Nathaniel. *Lyrics for the Bride of God* (New York: New Directions, 1975).

Tishby, Isaiah. *The Wisdom of the Zohar: An Anthology of Texts*, 3 vols., trans. David Goldstein (Oxford: Oxford University Press, 1989).

Unterman, Alan. *The Wisdom of Jewish Mystics* (New York: New Directions, 1976).

Vital, Hayyim ben Joseph. *The Tree of Life: The Palace of Adam Kadmon*, trans. Donald Wilder Menzi and Zwe Padeh (Northvale, NJ: Jason Aronson, 1999).

Weiner, Herbert. *9½ Mystics: The Kabbala Today* (New York: Collier Books, 1969).

Wineman, Aryeh. *Mystic Tales from the Zohar* (Philadelphia: The Jewish Publication Society, 1997).

———. *Beyond Appearances: Stories from the Kabbalistic Ethical Writings* (Philadelphia: Jewish Publication Society, 1988).

Wolfson, Elliot R. *Along the Path: Studies in Kabbalistic Myth, Symbolism, and Hermeneutics* (Albany: SUNY Press, 1995).

———. *Circle in the Square: Studies in the Use of Gender in Kabbalistic Symbolism* (Albany: SUNY Press, 1995).

———. *The Book of the Pomegranate: Moses de Leon's Sefer ha-rimmon* (Atlanta: Scholars Press, 1988).

Zohar al ha-Torah, 7 vols., second ed. (Jerusalem: Rabani Bavel, 1982).

ABOUT THE AUTHOR

David Rosenberg is the author of more than twenty books of poetry, translation and essays. Two of his volumes in the past decade have been named *New York Times'* "Notable Books of the Year," while a third, *A Poet's Bible,* was given the prestigious PEN/Book-of-the-Month Club Prize in 1992, the first major literary award for a biblical translation. His rendering of *The Book of J,* with commentary by Harold Bloom, was a national best-seller. After many years of study in Israel, Mr. Rosenberg was appointed editor-in-chief of the Jewish Publication Society. More recently, his 1973 volume, *The Necessity of Poetry,* was reissued, with a new introduction, in print and online Web formats. He now lives near the Florida Everglades with his wife, the writer Rhonda Rosenberg.